Truth is Truth even if no one believes it
A Lie is still a Lie even if everyone
believes it is the truth

Home
Within

KATHLEEN MONAGHAN

THE CHOIR PRESS

First published in the United Kingdom in 2020 by
The Choir Press

ISBN 978-1-78963-101-2

Table of Contents

Part Three

Introduction

HOME.

What does that mean to you?
Just some meanings from the dictionary:
A place where one lives, a residence.
A dwelling place together with the family.
An environment which offers security and happiness.
An institution where people are cared for.

Or:

H.O.M.E. – Habitat of Mixed Energies
H.O.M.E. – House of Many Errors

Searching for my home has been a long journey.
Home, with my mother, the children's home, foster home, children's home again, my first home as an adult, and countless others after that, none giving me the answer.
I had to look within …

This is a memoir in three parts, based on a girl being raised within two areas of the care system and how this affected her as she continued in her life after this.

This story follows her journey.

Part One is about Katy in her early years.

Part Two will follow Katy and occasionally popping up, along the way, Kate

Part Three, the conclusion, will follow Kate to the end of her journey to become Kathleen.

Kathleen was the name given to her by her mother. Once upon a time it was changed. Now she owns it once again.

An Old Gift

I lifted the old battered leather blue book; it smelled the same as always. I don't keep many things from my past, but I still had this: *What Katy Did* by Susan Coolidge. It's now nearly thirty-two years old.

Holding the book, I sighed, 'Seriously? What Katy did? The book on the *real* "Katy" would have been so different, so far along the scale from the one I was holding, but still a story and the truth.'

I have decided to tell 'Katy's' story for her. That 'Katy' lived within me for such a long time. I have now released her to heal. My inner child.

Stevie, one of the staff in the children's home I was staying in, handed me the book one Christmas and, in jest, said, 'If everyone knew what Katy really did, it would be a bestseller'. We both laughed as I was a bit of a mischief-maker. Little did he know his words still vibrate in my ears even now as I write.

No one knew my story.

What he meant was that the reports – our daily and weekly reports of our behaviour, mischiefs, truanting from school, coming in late, small things that were an everyday occurrence for staff and children in a home – would tell a different story to the one in the book.

What I meant was it was much darker than anything Susan Coolidge or this member of staff could ever have imagined.

Did the staff always get it right? No.

Are they to blame if there was a lack of training from their employer? Did they do their best in the circumstances? Did they just not see? Not because they looked away, but because the child wasn't dirty or hungry, she had a suntan from her recent trip abroad, she smiled and was polite, she did what she was told, came from a clean home where there was nothing but a loving family. That was the story portrayed – all lies. No trouble from her ... yet.

When a child has learned not to trust anyone, to fear adults, to be shown that when you do tell, even on small things, you're told, 'Don't lie', 'Don't speak back to your elders', 'Do as you are told or else', will they speak up?

No.

When a child learns that even the 'nice people' can hurt you, will they speak up?

No.

My trust had been so violated at the core of my relationship with the world and with 'family' that I trusted not a soul.

I had two faces which I put on for a long time: the sad, broken one which I hid as best as I could, and the strong one that faced the world when it got tough, hiding my pain because it was what protected me from more pain.

I was that child, now in a safe place away from the people that should have loved and cared for me as 'family', but who do I trust? Who do I tell? Why isn't someone asking me that one question that should have been asked and saying that they will protect me and keep me safe?

So I kept quiet and trusted no one, Adrenaline pumping constantly, waiting on the bad to come back. Smile, Katy – swear, act tough so you do not get bullied, go get into trouble, pretend you're like the other kids here, because they might think you're not a bad enough child to earn your place here, and then they might send you back there.

I wore the mask from then on for a long time after too. Disassociating from my past, avoidance of acknowledging my pain and smiling like a wee trooper.

It was how I coped. It was the only thing I knew how to do to protect myself from letting anyone see what was really going on. I didn't want anyone realising I was weak, felt dirty, felt pain, cried, hurt physically and feared everything. The feeling of abandonment and loss was the greatest next to the daily fear of surviving. That was masked so no one would see that weakness and attack me more. Sometimes it came automatically – maybe through practice or through my mind's action to protect me, I don't know. I just know it got me this far.

I am only telling my story in my words, my way.

I trust no one else to get them out there, done with rules, structure and people bending words or situations to suit their own agenda.

I have free will and I am a free spirit.

This book was not undertaken for me to play the 'victim', or for pity. I want none. I just wanted to take it all from my head and put it on paper. Acknowledge it one last time before I bury it.

It has taken me many years and many attempts to write this book throughout different parts of my life, so if you are reading and feeling twenty different personalities through the words, that's fine. I have evolved and changed through healing and the raw part is all here for you to see. I know I will never win any kind of accolade within the literary world, nor is that a goal, and I will not fit the category of being 'spiritually evolved' by many in that community but let me tell you again … I do not care.

I have delayed this project through embarrassment, shame, upsetting others. Too many excuses. The time has come to own this story, regardless.

One thing that is important to me, and to so many others, is music. It lifts the soul, it brings memories up, it empowers you, it gives you joy, it can have you in floods of tears.

So, I have gifted your ears some links within these pages if you choose to listen:

Part One – one song

Part Two and Part Three both have one song at the end of each chapter to let you as the reader experience something emotional within me that I maybe never conveyed clearly in my writing. It's not to everyone's taste in music but it personally resonated with me when I needed it.

There are also two songs dedicated to the people that mattered the most in this chaos, my mum and my grandad.

Enjoy.

The book has no real names of the people involved. Sometimes I use initials, and sometimes I have changed the name – either way, no real names remain. I will leave it up to you to decide if these characters are fictitious or not. Any resemblance to real persons living or dead is tough shit.

I will sugar-coat nothing in this book so others can feel comfortable. If you want a sugar coating, put the book down and try the baker's for a nice doughnut.

Much love,

Kathleen

Part One

———◄◦►———

CHAPTER 1

A Mother Forgotten

Searching the library of many memories in my head, I can't find the section on my mum, my dad, on our family home.

What did she look like? Did she play with me? Did I eat biscuits and watch TV with my brothers and sisters? Where was my daddy? Did we have fun? Did we feel safe?

No answers come, even looking at the one photograph I have now of my mum. No memories of her or my dad.

My first memory I can go back to is of being in the children's home:

I am lying on a sofa, strange faces gathering around me, pointing at my leg, asking if it hurt, a big old red blister on my inside thigh. Cats purring around me, walking along the edge of the sofa wondering who I was on their territory. It's a flat within a building, a small living room and the lady that's tending to me seems to be the matron or a nurse.

No previous memory of being in my family home whatsoever. None.

I'm now eating a custard cream as a reward for letting her clean my leg.

There is also a small, brief memory of playing outside, in a large garden, with other children and having a grapefruit for breakfast one morning and the tart taste.

Stories about that time spent in care surface much later in life when I asked and was told, 'You were fine – happy. We visited all the time.'

Stories from my grandad, 'You had whooping cough, weeping eczema, head lice, you were a mess, and you cried and screamed all the time.'

Maybe the memory of the sweet custard cream was so vivid because the rest was blocked out through the trauma I was living in. Memories still not available. Nothing.

I remember my kids at two years old. They knew me, my smell, and they would miss me if I left, they would cry, they would remember me.

No known facts at present about who made the decisions, who was involved. Was it my grandparents on my mum's side of the family? My father and all his family? No one stepped in to save us, so it seems – or did they? Too many different stories from too many people with their own view and heartache over what had happened, no files available, still no answer to my questions. These answers would come later in my life from my research.

Can I also be very clear that the disgust and contempt I felt for years at many people for the fact that since the day my mother died (at twenty-six years old of a heart attack, remember that, twenty-six, her life barely started as an adult), NO ONE, not one fucking person, kept her memory alive for me or my siblings. I can forgive my grandad in part for his silence because it was caused by severe grief and anger at the injustice of the whole situation but until I was older, I had nothing. It was like she never existed … a ghost.

She had died and no one decided to gather pictures of her in an album. No one spoke of her, her personality, her humour. Of how she was as a mother.

What was her wedding day like? What did she wear? Where are all the pictures of her?

An odd passing comment on how my sister looked like her. That was it. Say nothing and pretend it didn't happen. Or say nothing because of grief. Either way it was so wrong; a lack of information can be just as bad as giving the wrong information. You all got an A+ on both.

I was thirteen years old and my uncle found an old black-and-white photograph of my mum and copied it for me and my siblings. I treasured it for years

It is on the front cover of this book.

Now everyone gets to see who she was, she will not be forgotten.

I loved him so much and he was my godfather. I remember sitting on his knee as a child when he came to visit at New Year, combing his beard for him was a treat for me. He would blow raspberries on my face and neck, tickling me with his beard. He hugged me. He was warm and safe, a gentle giant of a man but stayed in his own lane with his own life.

My aunt (an ex -wife of my godfather who had been my mum's friend as they both dated my uncle and my father) had given me some information too when I was fifteen years old. Again, thank you – even all the smallest things that anyone ever said about her mattered greatly to me. They have both passed now, sadly.

Shame on every one of you that refused to be the first to speak about her, to lead the way on preserving a young woman's memory for her children. Would you have been happy if it was your daughter, sister or mother? Would you feel bereft in knowing that there was nothing ... ?

When my mum passed away suddenly on 29th June 1974, I went into the children's home described earlier. I believe I stayed in this children's home for around a year. The social work file is on its way as I write. A previous attempt many years ago to get this file came up with nothing. File lost. Notes are missing.

Not the people to be trusted, in my opinion.

*

It is now September 1975. I have a new family to live with.

The picture on the back cover of this book shows my new name, Katy, knitted onto my jumper, as Kathleen was too long. My name was changed, and so was my religion. I was now christened and a Catholic. No choices, just adults making decisions with no concern for my real name or my previous religion.

So, here's the story I grew up with: Mum was dead, and Dad was a drunk and never wanted the responsibility.

Not all true ... or was it though?

Nothing ever is when it comes to the stories of individuals not telling the truth, or not saying anything when they should. Taken collectively, you sometimes get a little nearer to the truth.

My eldest brother went to live with my maternal grandparents, and myself and my two siblings went to live in a children's home and now a new 'foster family'.

My dad had remarried after my mum passed.

I want to start off with a note.

Dear Willie Wheeler,

I had mixed emotions about loving you. I remember your rosy cheeks, amazing skin. The maker of the best chips I have ever had and the supplier of a biscuit tin that would choke a horse.

I saw your eyes as I grabbed three or four biscuits, maybe thinking I was greedy instead of just hungry. Saw the different reactions in your mood sometimes, not towards me, but at the fact that I had turned up alongside my brother and sister on our visits to your house full of excitement, about having some freedom to be myself – and all of this on top of you having two beautiful girls to take care of, and a drunken abusive husband. You cooked, cleaned and chatted, you never once asked us to do a thing. As a child, I never saw the woman that you were and still are: bravely protecting your children and doing everything in your power to love them and keep them safe. You brought them up to question everything and have a voice.

On the other hand, there was underlying confusion from me as a small child as to why you couldn't have been my mum too. I get it now.

From me, a distance towards your own children and yourself for years because of this, alongside the fact we were never allowed in younger years to spend any proper time getting to know each other. Time spent together was limited or controlled. The pain of feeling unloved and unwanted from so many areas hurt and I could not see this clearly. I tried again when I was older to form a bond when I was a mother, but underlying things prevented that, whether it was my issue or yours because of who you thought I was. It does not matter. I chose to stay away from everything in my past relating to family because of many things. Avoidance was my protection.

As a woman now, I understand the reason you made some decisions or statements. You made them for you and your family. I would do the same. When the shit hit the fan and you made a statement and a decision – one that I never understood why you said it and probably never forgave you for – as an older woman, now I get it.

Thank you for the many times you made me feel welcome in your home, fed and hugged me. Your association with others that caused this pain for me was your choice and it saddened me – the comments, the sides that looked to have been taken. Now I hope you understand why I keep a respectful distance.

CHAPTER 2

House of Many Errors

You know how you watch the adverts on the TV, take for instance the bread one, a young boy wandering home to a cosy house, chunk of bread with butter and tea. Loving smile from his parents because he fetched the loaf, as the tune that we all know plays in the background.

Then there's the dishwashing liquid one, children helping mother with the dishes and using the stuff that keeps your hands soft.

You have the picture.

Do these scenes exist outside the brain of the advertising executives?

No memories of arriving at my new home. Isn't it funny that even at two and three our memory is very clever, filing away all the shocks, hurt, anger, grief and archiving it till you get older and stronger or until you open that file, and boom!!!!!

Lucky children we were, taken from care and all kept together apart from the older one who went elsewhere and entering a lovely home with two working parents and some new brothers and sisters, yay!!! Bliss, we have a family ...

Prick! Pop ...

Ooh, someone just burst that bubble round that scene. Me, with a very large silver needle.

Family, yes, by blood through my father's side, but the connection and paper trail ended there.

One baby and two small girls, the baby yet to develop his personality and the girls already starting to develop theirs, wondering what the hell was going on: 'You're my mummy now? Where's my real mummy?' Crying and confused, no doubt. I'm surmising as I remember nothing of going there.

The pictures tell a tale: ribbons in the hair and fresh new clothes, me smiling for the camera, my sister looking lost and the baby unaware, always a picture of us all together, the three of us, 'his three', as we were called. How many of the 'family' all together? How many not staged for memories of this perfect opportunity we were so blessed to have from this lovely family?

I look through my box of photos, my children, faces different in every single one, expressing themselves even when I ask, 'Sit like this', or 'Do a surprised face', their own little personalities shine through and nothing looks staged. They acted on their own feelings: caught in a moment, licking chocolate from a spoon and scrunching up newspaper and their hands all black, a mischievous look that says, 'I'm too young to know what I'm doing, but it's fun'. Pictures of surrounding family hugging them, hushing them to sleep, pushing them on a swing.

So different to the few I have.

'Sit here, Katy.'

'Do this, Katy.'

'Smile for the camera, Katy.'

Records of how happy it looked.

The camera never lies.

As I sit and look through my box of pictures from my childhood which were given by relatives, an odd few from the foster family, a particular one of me and my brother and sister, on holiday, standing at the edge of the swimming pool, staged, no splashing in the water, standing still – 'Smile for the camera'. My hands crossed in front of my private space. Smile not quite reaching the corners of my eyes. Hand that to a body language expert and let's see what they say …

Memories arise, but we will keep that for another chapter.

Thinking of my children and thinking of my childhood is such a massive jump on the scale from selfless unconditional love to fear and horror.

Let me now introduce this new family I now had:

FM – Foster Mother – my father's sister
FF – Foster Father
FS – Foster Sister
BFB – Bully Foster Brother
PFB – You will need to wait on this one for now.

My mind floats back to my (FM) foster mother's voice. 'Fanny Adams,' she screams. 'In here!' My adrenaline is pumping, legs are shaking and I think I'm about to wet myself. I'm thinking, what now, what have I done now, my mind racing over the checklist of my chores. I walk to the living room to her chair where she sits at the fireplace, her finger giving the 'come here' motion. 'Closer!' she shouts. I can hardly put one foot in front of the other because I know what's coming. My brain is saying, run, danger, and my body is moving forwards because you obeyed her, not your gut instinct, not your natural reaction to run ... Her.

Slap ... side of my leg stinging, I wince as non-responsively as I can so as it does not irritate her further, and the tears start flowing but they are steady, no bawling, because crying louder got you another. I take my punishment with quiet sobs and a head hung, no eye contact to stare her out. 'Room!' she screams.

What had I done, you ask? Stole from her? Ripped wallpaper off, drew on the walls, broken an expensive vase? No, because you didn't do that sort of thing; you behaved. You got punished for not abiding by her rules. You got punished because you messed up one of her tasks or it just wasn't done to her standards. Or you got punished just because she could.

Going to the kitchen window on the way to my room I lifted the net curtain. My friends had been waiting on me to go out to play. I gestured for them to go. They could see I'd been crying again. 'You kept in again?' they mouthed. I nodded, they left, nothing new here.

I went to my room as ordered and cried into the pillow so she couldn't hear me. I berated myself for being so stupid and missing something. I had left food particles at the side of the dish drainer where it met the tray underneath it – I didn't see them. I had done everything else: the dishes, worktops, floor, bleached the cloth. Stupid, stupid me. Now I wasn't going out to play. Now I had to sit in my room with no light on. No music, no TV, just read a book from the bookshelf in the hall if I was lucky. The same books I had memorised because I was always in that room reading them, not out playing. She saw it as an educational extra; it felt like a prison. The room had a lock outside, high up. It would be locked from the outside sometimes.

I hated her nicknames and I remember at times saying under my breath, my name is fucking 'Katy', but no one heard. My face was in the pillow, hiding my grief and anger. My spirit was still strong even at a young age, albeit silent in public.

Oh yes, I slipped in the odd silent swearword, even at a young age from around nine or ten. That has never left me and probably never will, unless someone can come up with a better word than 'fuck' to describe a multitude of emotions and events. I still love dropping the odd one into a conversation and seeing people's reactions.

Respectful family we had, you know ...

The posh voice only existed for the outsiders, the general public. In this house swearing was undertaken and I heard it on the street and from my friends. I used to see blatant hypocrisy as FM answered the telephone in her ever-so-polite voice to the caller when she had just been screaming abuse at me two minutes before in her not-so-polite voice.

Crying all the time was the norm from me. I was called 'Greeting Face'. I didn't know then that crying releases toxins from anger and negativity and it waters that little acorn too, nourishes it with water ...

Name-calling in this house was the norm. I had Fanny Adams, Lady, and Greeting Face to start with, and the best one they made for me was Haggy Doo the Black Haggis. This was from a radio show we had heard on a holiday in Scotland.

Why did I get this horrible demeaning nickname? Because I hated getting washed. I hated using the cloth in the bathroom to wash myself properly. I flicked the water around my ears and face. The reason is clear for me, and you will understand soon. To them, I was just dirty. As for the other names, I'm not aware of why she used them, but Haggy Doo was one that I understood and accepted. Who was the smart, dirty child here?

We had one bath a week, shared with everyone else. One after the other, scummy water, younger brother usually urinated in it for badness, and I wasn't allowed to wash my hair midweek. We were 'dirty' because you gave us no other option, dear FM. They were your rules.

I had long hair when I was younger. FM would come up to wash it and she would throw the jug of water over my face. If I cried or tried to wipe the water away, she would grab me and push me under the water. One time I panicked so badly I grabbed on to her and nearly pulled her into the bath. She went downstairs, complaining to whoever would listen that I had soaked her and was 'greeting' again for nothing.

My kids have never feared water. I bathed them gently and made sure if any water ran in their eyes that I had a nearby cloth. Bath times were fun times, and my kids usually refused to come out into the warm towel and pyjamas that I had on the radiator for them.

I was made to stand with no towel in a cold bath, my hair being combed roughly, taking the tugs out in yanks. No conditioner. The older FS would sometimes be sent to do this, and she was a little gentler, using an afro comb with wider prongs. FM had no sense of empathy: she tugged and pulled, getting herself worked up and angry because she had to do this for me.

You also got the visual prompt or finger gesture of 'come here', no conversation, when you came in from out playing, if you got out in the first place. This was one of FM's other ritual punishments: 'You're kept in.'

On returning from a rare night out playing one summer night, I walked towards her, legs shaking as usual, adrenaline pumping and my mind racing just waiting on the barrage of prying questions. 'Where were you? Who were you with?' I answered and then she would nonchalantly say 'Okay' and wave her hand dismissively. I walked away with urine dribbling down my legs, no slap but the same feelings of terror. Conditioned to feel the fear.

Digital watches were pre-set when they were gifted as a birthday present when I was older. I would arrive home, checking my watch, releasing my held-in breath as I checked that it was 7.57 pm.

'You're late!' she would scream, I would say nothing. She asked what time my watch was at. '7.59,' I would reply, fear now returning. 'Well, your watch is wrong. You are in for a week for being irresponsible and not keeping your watch at the correct time.' (It was the summer holidays and that was the only reason I was allowed out to this time in the first place.)

As I got older and started to understand that this family situation was not the norm, I ran away on about five occasions overnight, staying at friends' houses, hiding. I always got found. I was a dreamer, not a planner. When I was growing up, I started to see other families and how they lived together, other parents' reactions and interactions with their kids. I started to realise how toxic this family was.

We had some friends who stayed in the building where we lived, and their parents were lovely. Of course, I couldn't run away to their houses but I'm sure they would have helped me if I'd asked. But I was too terrified of the outcome if they took me back there and I disgraced her. This stopped me doing most of the things I wanted to do – fear. She had ingrained it into me so deep I still thought she could see and know everything I was doing, even when she wasn't there.

My friend's mum was so loving, worked with people who

had special needs and ran a family home on her own, attractive and slim. She was welcoming when you went to her home and you got anything she had to share. FM looked down her nose at her.

Another family lived up the stairs and my other friend waited with anticipation every Friday on her dad coming around the corner. She would rush to check his pockets for a 'Friday piece' – this was usually a bar of chocolate. I watched him laugh at her delight and give her a hug. I felt so sad, but joyous for her.

A friend next door who I attended music lessons with had such a proactive father. He took the time to help us practise our instruments, spoke about books and other random things. He was an educated man with a wry sense of humour and the cheekiest smile, always wanting the best for everyone. Her mum was outspoken but kind, and she painted her nails in lots of different colours. She took time to love and defend her children. Nice people.

I was allowed next door to the neighbour's house sometimes at their request, to practise music, even though sometimes we just played in the room or went on the computer to play The Hobbit. There was no fuss or strict rules.

Freedom.

They had a cat and FM told me not to touch it as it was dirty. I deliberately stroked her every day – her fur was soft, and her purring was comforting. She sat on the kitchen window ledge as I passed. The cat probably never liked FM either. Animals and kids sense shit people.

None of my friends liked FM.

She demanded to be called by her title of Mrs _____ unlike the other parents, who were happy to be called by their first names. People saw right through her persona of 'I am better than all of you', delusions of grandeur spewing from her pores. FM frowned upon everyone around her. Judging away without acknowledging what they could clearly see about who she was.

Running away from this house was a total farce. I had no

food, money or a plan of where to go and the FM and her family went around the doors like the Gestapo.

A few times I arrived at my dad's house, hoping he would let me stay with him, and got a hot cup of tea before the FM dragged me out, nipping my arm as she held it. She would be grinding her teeth through her fake smile, her ever-popular public face showing but her mask slipping because of her anger at my insolence.

My dad looked on with such pain and helplessness in his face. I pleaded to him with my eyes and saw the tears run down his face. He did nothing, and I hated him at that moment. The next day he would be back on the drink. That was his answer – use the alcohol to numb his guilt. I felt let down again that he never stood up to her, and I knew he was weak. His actions then affected his new family and I carried that guilt of dragging them into it. I never meant for anyone else to get hurt. I just wanted away from that house.

On one occasion I ran away because of keys. Fucking keys!

When you got to a certain age in this house, you were awarded with a set of keys to let yourself in after school as FM was now full-time at work. You used them to let yourself in after being out at night too because FM hated answering the bell. Summer nights where I lived were usually full of local kids playing British Bulldog, Kick the Can, Two-Man Hunt. Large expanses of grass gave us this area to let our imaginations run wild. The way childhood should be.

On a night that I did get out to play, during the summer holidays, it was time to go home, 7.55pm. I was soaked because we'd had a water balloon fight. Suddenly I realised that there were no keys in my pocket. My anxiety peaked as I had to make the decision to be late and try and find them, or to go and admit I had lost them. Either choice was bad. I walked quickly along to the door, head going one hundred miles an hour, thinking of what was going to happen now. I rang the bell with my shaking hands and BFB answered. He asked, 'Where's your keys?'

'I've lost them,' I said quietly, and a slap to the side of my head ensued. 'Get back out and look for them,' he said, then ranted as he closed the door. I felt relieved it was him.

I ran back to the area where I had been playing. The other kids all helped me look for them, me in tears, saying 'Aww no, I'm going to get such a doon' (doon is a Glaswegian word for a beating). I was soaked through to the skin because of the water fight and the night air coming down, and now I was shivering. It was now near 10 pm and getting dark, and some of the other kids had gone home, some stayed, outside in the dark, no adult there. This was a scene brought about by the person that would not let me stay out after 8 pm in the summer holidays. Here I was, now alone in the dark, except from the company of a friend who would take the wrath from her mother because she was helping a friend. A mother, who would ultimately understand her and praise her for staying with me, instead of giving her a beating for being late home.

As if on cue, FM appeared, saying, 'Right, you, upstairs.' (She wouldn't hit me in front of anyone.) I walked with the usual dribble forming between my legs, and my friend stood watching my FM with contempt on her face, and a look of pity for me.

When we got inside the house, FM said nothing apart from 'Bed'. I went up the stairs and put the wet clothes in the washing basket and went to bed, cold and scared of what was coming. Maybe this time she understood it wasn't my fault and I would just have to get new keys cut. Something told me in my gut that was never going to happen. I barely slept, awaiting her wrath.

The next day I was awakened at 7 am by FM dragging me from my bed, 'Get the clothes out the dirty washing and put them back on. Get back out and look for your keys.'

Not a crumb of breakfast, wet clothes sticking to my skin. It was raining. I walked over and over the grass I'd been playing on the night before. I was soaked and hungry, tears spilling down my face. The ground had been covered over and over the night before. I'd had enough of FM; she was a bully. I started to walk towards a *friend's house, and then ran in a sprint in case FM saw me from her car on the way to work, and I did not stop until I got there. I had no breath by the time I had reached her door through running so fast and adrenaline from the panic of what I was doing.*

She opened the door to my frantic chapping (knocking), still in her nightgown, half asleep. One look from her at the tears starting to build in my eyes and the soaked clothes, and she took me in without question and ran me a bath to warm up in and then made me toast and tea. Angel.

I stayed away for one night at her home. Her mother never questioned it because most of the kids had friends to stay over in the holidays. The next day, around teatime, I was walking along the main road, watching for anyone looking for me. Shit. I had been spotted.

I started running like a gazelle from a lion as I saw BFB and FF walking towards us. I ran around the back of a building at the motorway and hid in bushes. The next thing I felt was a thud to my ankle that was slightly sticking out the bush. I'd been caught and BFB decided to stamp on my ankle. I was dragged by the hair back to the street, tears and snot on my face, hobbling on my ankle. My friends stood watching, some in tears. My ankle was starting to swell and turn black. No one saw that. All hidden under thick nice white school socks the next day. Nothing to see here, folks.

No sign of a caring word, like 'Hey, are you okay? We've been worried about you. Come home and we can sort it.' Not a chance.

Dragged indoors, I was sent up for a bath, scalding hot. Neat Savlon liquid from a bottle was poured over me, running into my eyes, stinging them, dribbling into my mouth. I was told to get scrubbed as I was a 'dirty, filthy runaway'. Welcome home, 'Katy'. Within this moment though, I found the joy in having a bath to myself.

One split second of joy amongst the terror. To this day, even in chaos or drama, I can still find one thing to be positive about. That's a gift.

My school uniform lay out on the bed, for the new term was

starting the next day. At least I'd get to see my friends who I had missed through the summer. I always said nothing about my home life to my schoolfriends, pretending everything was okay. No story to tell. Just smile, Katy. It was like I had two different lives.

There was no interview by anyone, no social workers, no police. Why did these social workers never come out after I had run away? Answers for this will come later.

Mental torment was daily; you never knew what was coming or what for. You could be sitting in your room, grounded again for anything, and FM would come in and put the light on. I'd put my book down and await her wrath. I was tired of squinting at the book in the fading light from the window anyway. We weren't allowed to waste electricity in this house, while she sat downstairs in front of a cosy electric fire, spinning the electricity meter like Pete Burns on stage with his hit song.

Wardrobe doors would be opened and folded jumpers from the shelves would be pulled out. 'Not tidy enough!' she would scream. Games would be pulled from under the sheet on the bed and thrown across the room. 'Do you realise these are family games? They are not yours!' she would shout. 'How dare you disrespect them!' she would say, as she threw the box on the floor.

The Connect 4 plastic markers were messy, the Monopoly pieces were untidy, and the money was mixed up. I hadn't even played them. But it was my fault because they were under the double bed I shared with my sister, and they were messy. Not sure she quite got the word 'games'.

Saturdays were such fun for young people: *Swap Shop* on TV, long lie-ins, hanging out with friends because there was no school ... Pop! There goes that bubble around that little fantasy again. The silver needle returns.

Saturdays in this environment were shopping days, cleaning days, no different from the other days but more intense.

Washing other people's shit off the toilet bowl with bleach. No gloves. Hand right down and up around the bend. If I had any cuts on my hand, they would sting with the bleach.

Another memory appears. The monthly food-shopping trips to the supermarket. The strip lighting in the supermarket would hurt my eyes and a headache then ensued. I would tell FM my head was sore. She ignored me. I would then feel sick with the pain and start to cry. She would tell me children did not get headaches. She would tell me to stop my crying and get to bed, adding that if I had such a bad headache then I would not want dinner. I lay in my bed in the dark, hungry and in pain. No one came to check if I was okay. My sister would come in later and cuddle up with me, would let me put my cold feet between her warm legs. Years later while I had an MRI for another issue, I was diagnosed with a Chiari malformation at the base of my brain. It caused the excruciating headaches and nausea. It had been there since I was born.

On most other days at the weekend, cupboards were opened and the tins to be arranged and wiped, skirting boards around the room to be cleaned, the freezer (a massive one, the kind you see in shops) defrosted – and no gloves, so your hands got ice burn. FM took pride in that freezer, filled twice a year by the butcher, showing off her wealth as she liked to do. That fostering payment certainly came in handy for a few steaks and some fine Sunday brisket.

The cooker was pulled out and cleaned at the sides and the back and underneath, a slap to the head here and there if it wasn't getting done fast enough or to her standards, or because it was your fault that the stain was there because you had put the dinner on the other day, and it had spilled over and burned. Tins in the cupboard were lined up in order, and the towels on the rail in the bathroom perfectly folded.

I watched a film years later and it brought all this back. It was called *Sleeping with the Enemy*.

I call it referred OCD, she looked around for imaginary dirt and things to be obsessively cleaned and she referred it out. She needed control in everything.

One time she was angry about the veranda outside her living room being cluttered with plants that FF tended to. In her rage she started moving them and dropping soil. FF ran towards her and grabbed his tomato plants and told her to leave them. An argument ensued and I saw him having to drag her in from the veranda. She was like a woman possessed. I sat on the sofa, terrified at what was going on but wanting him to slap her, beat her. See how she liked it. He never did. He fixed his plants and went to the pub. Was I wrong to want to see her hurt and know how that feels?

She went on to tell others he was losing his mind. Said he had dragged her by the hair, and he was doing forward rolls in the bottom bunk bed. Making him look like a crazy man whilst deflecting from her own behaviour, a usual tactic of hers. Berating someone else was the norm in this house. Even her husband endured this.

Did she do the same with her own kids? I don't know, but I remember my sister questioning why we had to do this; she was brave sometimes. After a backhander it was explained to her that her own children were busy studying for their future and one day we would get fewer chores when we were in the same position. Until then it was our duty. Didn't we realise we were learning how to organise a clean home for our future?

Everything she made us do she justified by telling us it was for our benefit.

Did I feel like Cinderella? A little, but this isn't a tale of 'poor me, all my chores'. Other people I know had strict parents and they helped the family with chores, but they also got to play. I'm sure there are others that have this same experience or worse. The only difference was I was not waiting for Prince Charming either, because we find out later the charming ones are not what they seem.

The reason for explaining the cleaning frenzy part, the physical and mental abuse from FM, is to show the control, the control that facilitated fear and obedience, which had been ingrained in me for a very long time. To show I was living in FM's enclosure of fear daily, waiting for FM to strike, or someone else to do much worse . . .

CHAPTER 3

Control Over Food

Cupboards full of tins and packets, freezer full of food. Did we get fed? Yes, but she chose what, how much and when. Yet when visitors were at her home for parties or celebrations she pulled out all the stops. The alcohol flowing freely, then her making derisive comments afterwards about anyone that got drunk on her alcohol and made an arse of themselves.

My memory shifts to yesterday, my daughter coming in from school, hardly getting a 'Hey Mamma' out before her head's in the fridge, seeing what she fancies, and then looking in the drawer for a treat. Or my friends coming to the house with their kids to visit and tasting the baking, or the soup, helping themselves to a bowl, or taking some home because I made too much. Everyone fed with no guilt, normality. Food is there for nourishment, to be shared, made with love. I am grateful I never ended up with any eating disorder from her behaviour.

You ate what was on your plate, you did not leave that table until you had finished. Sometimes a bottle of brown sauce was on the table and I wanted to put some over my food to take the taste away, but that was insulting to her cooking, even though she rarely cooked, the task instead being undertaken by my sister or me, so the same bottle of sauce sat there, only used by the adults, only there for show to let everyone know we could afford that brand.

Now, there was no give and take, no hiding the peas amongst the good parts. You ate, and you ate everything, or else.

The piece of fat off the steak lay on my plate, fat and congealed like a witchery grub. I had cut it off, pushed it to the side and wolfed down the hot mixed vegetables, full of broad beans and green beans, then shovelled the boiled-to-death potatoes down next, thinking, 'Right, that's the shit stuff out the way. Now I could enjoy my steak.' Steak gone, I went to get up from my chair now that the elders were leaving the table. I lifted my plate. She saw the fat. Fuck!

'You're not finished, lady'. Sitting back down, I started to slice the fat into small pieces, the grease coating the roof of my mouth as I chewed quickly, trying to swallow. Don't gag, I told myself, just swallow and pretend it's something nice. She sat and watched for the ten minutes it took me to force this down my throat and then said, 'Room.' I knew I was grounded for being ungrateful for my steak.

Do you know how many kids in those days got steak? We were privileged, you know. What an ungrateful urchin I was. Oliver Twist only got gruel.

The times that she left the table while I was still eating my food, I had a hanky up my sleeve prepared to fill it with anything that was disgusting. I would wrap the offending food in the tissue and hide it down my trousers, my pants half wet with soggy veg. I would then hide it under the kitchen sink when I was doing the dishes or under my bed until I could get it out of the house.

It was disgusting. Sometimes if I forgot about it or could not get it out without her prying eyes, it would go mouldy and smell. There was no scraping the leftovers in the bin, the bin was checked. Yes, she checked the bin to see who had left anything. FM was obsessed over wasted food.

Another occasion comes to mind as I have just told the steak fat story. Packet powdered cheesy pasta, a well-known orange packet...

It was cold and powdery, smelled like sick and I struggled to eat it. I was in tears, refusing to eat it, taking tiny bits. Her patience ran out and I was left at the table with FF, who usually sat at the dinner table later than us when he arrived in from work.

He had been instructed to make sure I ate it. He was pissed off and was desperate to go and relax after a working day and put his feet up for a snooze and a cigarette. 'Just get it ate,' he said. I pleaded with my eyes, hoping he would see I was struggling. No chance!

He lifted up handfuls of it and forced it in my mouth. I swallowed in pure shock, fear overtaking, and fear of what would happen if I disobeyed him and didn't swallow. He was angry at being told what to do by her again, and as usual it was directed at me.

He looked smug. 'There, it wasn't that hard, was it? Now wash the dishes and get to your bed!'

Ready . . . aim . . . fire . . . the cheesy pasta decided along with the rest of the contents of my stomach it wanted to pay him a visit.

Lumps of orange pasta and sauce covered his trousers and velour slippers. It was worth the slap from him. I went up the stairs to my bed that night with a win and some joy in my heart. You may try to control me but what goes in my mouth and out the other end can never be controlled.

Packets and packets of biscuits were stacked up in the cupboard. Counted like the slices of bread.

Coming in from school hungry, I'd take a rich tea biscuit, because they were easier to miss, spoon some icing sugar on it and cram the whole thing in my mouth. It stuck to the roof of my mouth and melted slowly, sweet and crunchy. I would sit on the floor of the kitchen savouring each bite. It was stealing and I knew it was, but I was hungry and knew I would be in trouble if I got caught. I was so hungry I would have taken any punishment.

I did get caught once. Biscuits . . .

The words still make my sister and I give a knowing glance and a snigger to each other when we mention it because I got her into trouble over this.

I had taken a full pack of biscuits from the bundle in the cupboard. FM had more than one pack in amongst the other packs. She won't miss this one packet out of nine. How stupid was I?

I went under the bed, where I had hidden the full pack, and pulled out two biscuits before my sister came into the room. 'Here you go, we are allowed one.' Mine was done in two bites. She savoured hers. My sister was sitting on the bed munching the biscuit when FM entered the room. 'Where did you get that from?' she screamed. My sister gave a look of horror at me and I pleaded with my eyes for her not to tell. 'We stole them,' my sister said. 'It was my idea.'

Slap. 'You're both in for a week. Get to bed!' I was distraught at my sister being punished. She did this often – she always had my back.

In this house nothing was ever private. FM went through drawers and into schoolbags, looked under the mattress. She was always looking to find something. I had a small amount of money hidden in her wardrobe. She never found it.

My sister knew I had it there. I told my sister I had saved it from cleaning the close (the entrance to the shared flats, which residents were responsible for cleaning on a weekly rota) for old Mrs Whoever, and I had taken a few glass cheques (or gingeys as they're known in Glasgow, the returnable glass bottles worth 5p each upon return) back to the shops from people's houses that couldn't be bothered or were too embarrassed to do so. If you can imagine the faces of glee from the local kids as they clinked along with a bag full, after going around chapping neighbour's doors collecting these from people for nothing, knowing they had money to get back from the shop to then buy sweeties. Most adults were too embarrassed or lazy to be returning them.

I also used to ask the local football supporters parking their car near my house, 'Hey, mister, can I watch your car?' A very famous Glasgow team had their ground nearby, and a lot of the kids in the area did this on match days. They would promise us 10p and would say they would give you it when they got back. I would stand there the full time they were away watching their team play, making sure no one broke into their car. As I got older and wiser, I only returned to the car when the game finished and collected my money, while in between playing in the lifts in the high-rise flats while my friends raced me up the stairwell.

That earned me extra money for treats from the shop so I would not look like the odd one out in my group.

I was warned by the FM not to do it as it was like begging, but I did. All the other kids were doing it. I wanted to be like them.

But saying where I got most of my hidden money from was not an option.

If I had said that PFB had given it to me, he would have denied it and then I would have been accused of being a thief. Then it would be his word against mine and I was never going to win. I did not get pocket money, so where did I get it from? I said nothing, because staying quiet was the lesser of two evils – the consequences of being labelled a thief were worse. No voice. Just do as you are told. He was your elder; you did not talk back to your elders.

Two weeks later I used some of this money I had hidden to buy another pack of biscuits from the local shop to replace the stolen ones and my sister and I went to FM, explaining I had cleaned someone's close to earn money. We thought if we replaced the biscuits, she would forgive us. She took the biscuits and dropped them in the bin beside her chair. And sent us both back up the stairs to our room. Letting us know that she was still in control, as always.

I was a thief because I was hungry, and now I was also a liar, having to lie about where the money came from. Maybe you should ask your son ... ?

CHAPTER 4

The Rules

So it has already become clear, FM ruled the roost, FF did what he had to do to support the family and he stepped in when told.

He stepped in with physical punishment and you got that from him when he was not ignoring you. Indifferent or sleeping, drank himself stupid on a Friday in the pub after work. He came in from work, ate dinner and slept on his chair. Smoked away on his cigarettes one after another and saved the coupons from them in a bundle next to his chair. On weekends he tended to his plants and fed the birds some nuts. He would teach us the names of the birds landing on the nut cage. He would laugh like a schoolboy at the names 'blue tit' and 'great tit'. On holiday, he would be enjoying a bit more freedom to drink and he would be half-drunk most of the time. He would give us an extra 50p if our daily quota of a pound had run out.

I was not brave enough to question but boy was FM shit at maths. Our chores, we were told, would earn us a pound a week to be put in our 'holiday money' to spend as we wished.

So, 52 weeks = £52, right?

No.

Her logic was 14 days away on holiday = 2 weeks of £1 per day

So, £14.

Bastards!

I was too young and too scared to question it. FF would tell us to use the 1p and 2p machines in the arcades to try stretch our money out and win extra money. Promoting gambling to children whilst half-cut on booze? Too funny! This was the only time I ever saw any sort of resonance of his real personality, but it seemed sad, to be honest.

There was never any conversation or quality time from him like my friend's dad next door. He was distant and uninvolved till he was pushed to get involved.

The other issue I had with him was his weird spying if I had been sent to my room or my sister and I were in bed. We would be told to put the lights out, no music, etc. Sometimes there would still be light coming in from the window and we would not be tired so we would read books near the window on my side of the bed, or we had a small torch under the covers.

Creak.

The second stair always made this noise. My hearing was so sharp because of the adrenaline and constant state of fear. My sister used to call me 'Batfink', a children's cartoon character who had super-sensory hearing.

FF was coming up the stairs. He would walk up the stairs as quietly as he could, hoping that we could not hear him, then burst into the room. By then the torch would be off and we would be lying there pretending to sleep. The book would be hidden under the bed. My sister and I laughed at him for being so stupid not to realise that nearly every time he tried to catch us, he failed. I was tuned in to every sound, always on high alert.

Other times we did get caught talking because he would stand outside our room door after he had been to the bathroom.

FF would be standing silent for ages. I would say, 'He must be gone by now.' We would start chatting, thinking he was away, and he would, again, open the door. 'Right, you two, get tae sleep.' He would tell the FM. We were grounded the next day. For talking!

What the fuck did he think we were doing? Planning a bank robbery?

He was a functioning drunk, yet we were stopped having visits to my grandparents' house or my dad's house, as they had issues with drink – hypocrisy at its highest.

My head returns to the past again when I speak of him. One time he did cross a line. Went right over the fucking line till the end of the road and around the corner to a dark place. Bastard!

I am in my maths class in secondary school. I cannot sit against the school chair because the bruises hurt and the dried blood from my wounds on my back was sticking to my school shirt.

I had been given the 'belt' the night before from the FF when FM was at a crime prevention meeting for the neighbourhood. How ironic. FM had left instructions for me to 'be dealt with'.

I was taken to my room and when he instructed me to pull my trousers down and lay face down on the bed, I was thirteen years old at this point.

Not the usual belt from the cupboard, the one with no buckle. The belt came off his trousers this time. He was busy. That set him off. Being told what to do by her, again, always did. Face full of rage as he struggled to pull it from the belt loops.

The first blow struck across my bare bottom. I turned to look at him, relief washing over me that I really was getting the belt and nothing else. His face was contorted with rage and he struck blow after blow, and the belt buckle caught my back.

He stopped eventually, anger sated.

I was left to pull my trousers up and told to get to bed.

I had held in my tears and my screams till he left the room. Sitting there gulping and sobbing, I was in total shock at what he had just done, but again, finding the positive in the fact it was only the belt my arse had gotten … I had to bury my face under my pillow so he could not hear me crying in case he came back up angrier and hit me again.

My sister came home that night and I lifted my nightdress and showed her the welts, bruising and cuts on me from my shoulders down to the back of my knees. She went mad and tried to voice her anger at this, but it did not work in this house

She tried to go to the hall to grab the phone to call the police and was wrestled to the ground by FM. BFB then got involved and started to hit her with the handle of the old heavy Bakelite rotary-dial phone that sat in the hall on the telephone table.

I watched from behind the wall at the top of the stairs, terrified at what I was seeing, the chaos ensuing down below and the cries of my sister. Every time I shared or asked for help, somebody got hurt. I was in tears. I needed to stop pulling other people into my pain. Just keep quiet, Katy . . .

I cuddled into my sister that night, saying sorry over and over for her hurt. She left that house soon after.

The next day at school I was ordered out from class and my guidance teacher was called because I was being unruly. Not ever had I gotten into trouble. Me, unruly? I was always a model pupil in case they reported back to FM.

The maths teacher was being a dick.

I followed my guidance teacher to his office for a chat and he laughed as he asked what I had done. I said nothing, hanging my head as I turned around and lifted my skirt.

His smile left his face; he left his office and returned with the head teacher. They called the local social work team.

The social worker arrived in his blue Puffa jacket, black curly messy hair and a funny eye. I had never seen him before.

I was asked to show my injuries to him. I then tried to open my shirt, but the guidance teacher stepped in as he was aware there was a young woman in a private office with three grown men, about to undress. I was just needing someone to see the injuries properly. I did not care if I had to stand naked. I wanted to be away from there, and this was my chance, surely. They would listen to all the other stuff if they saw this.

The social worker then took me back to the foster home and I was sent upstairs, to my room, my prison.

I do not know what was discussed, and then he left.

I heard the front door close and the urine started to dribble down my legs. I knew FM would come for me.

She did.

I was given another beating for 'grassing'.

*'You could have got your father the jail!' was screamed as she
rained her blows upon me.*

*After a while she came up and ordered me into a bath -scalding
hot water and Savlon again. She scrubbed at the cuts on my back
with the Savlon and a nail brush. She had to be seen attending to
my wounds, didn't she ...*

Procedure? Protection of children? No report of assault to
the police?

No safe space, no private interview. Taken back to the scene
of the crime and left with the abusers.

*'Thanks for fuck all, you messy-haired, wonky-eyed tramp,' I had
fumed under my breath as I sat there on the bed with tears in my
eyes from the scrubbing in the bath.*

The visits were sparse over the years in this foster
placement under the care of the social work department –
and a social worker just witnessed the marks of abuse in a
child and walked away. I wish they had taken off their
rose-tinted filter of this situation and done their job correctly
and followed the rules. They should have had the instinct to
see right through FM's mask and deliberate manipulation of
the whole meeting and protect the children that needed it.
But she was good, eloquent, educated, polite. She fooled lots
of people. FM controlling the whole staged scenario, bumping
her gums about how we all had social activities, music lessons
and holidays.

Awards and trophies shown, all sitting on her fireplace for
show and tell. Let's not forget the box of staged photos, detailing
our journey, that sat in a drawer and was fished out for
reference. The trophies were from a local youth club that she
was happy to farm us out to an odd night a week. Sometimes
she came and helped with the tuck shop. We got to spend her
money on those nights because she couldn't run the tuck shop
and leave us not having anything. On the other nights, we did
without. She had to show herself to be part of the community,
an upstanding member who had taken in these poor children

and gave them such a lovely life instead or rotting in a care home. Who the fuck was she trying to kid?

She bullied and organised anyone weaker than herself. Not many people liked her.

I remember one rare visit from the social work department, when everything was staged as usual. It was the same when anyone came to this house. There were six kids and two adults in a small house. No mess. Children sat on the sofa, scrubbed and quiet, the finery brought out and our clothes pressed to precision for the day. Good china and chocolate biscuits on the table. All staged as a perfect picture of family life.

'Do you like it here'? The social worker would ask. We nodded at her as we watched FM glare across the room at us, daring us to keep quiet. Conditioned to act and answer as she wanted us to do.

That was all we got asked.

After we all had nodded, eyes wide with fear at this questioning from a stranger, we were sent to our rooms again as the social worker finished her 'report'; that way we could not see them out to the door, or even answer it to them. Control on who we were left alone with when it suited her agenda to keep up appearances.

Six kids, no mess.

The reality should have been that the three kids in her care would run in and grab a biscuit from the plate, said hello, wave and run back out – not interested in reports or who you were, too busy being young and happy. The reality should have been that the social workers were trained to ask the important questions and recognise bullshit.

The only thing that I seemed to remember that was consistent was that we had a yearly medical, boxes ticked again. No marks, correct weight and height. The doctor forgot to look under my groomed hair at the lumps on my head that I had got from FM banging the brush on my skull if I moved when she was doing my hair. One time the brush snapped into two pieces because she hit me so hard. He missed the lump with a chip on the left side of my forehead where I had fallen against a wall. I had tripped and nearly knocked myself out. A massive egg on my forehead and I felt dizzy.

'Get to your bed for screaming and embarrassing me in front of the neighbours,' she spat. No ice. There was a chunk of my front skull missing and nothing done to help me. It's still missing, a reminder of her 'care'.

FM was very smart before visits from outsiders or family: she would know when they were coming, softened from her usual demeanour, no slaps. We knew something had changed but did not really know what.

In the case of the running-away episodes, she had a duty to inform the social work department that the children in her care were missing. She never did. The assault with the belt was reported by the school. What did they do? Fuck all ... This incident of failure left me in a seriously worse position than I had been before.

The one saving grace was that one social worker did do his job to a certain extent, and we can discuss that later in another chapter. But it was still not enough. The damage had been done by then.

CHAPTER 5

Control, Conditioning and Angels

Everyone did what they were told with no questions asked. Control was at the centre.

Nobody could question FM's authority, and if you did then woe betide you.

Christmas and birthdays were under her control. 'Write a letter to Santa with the things you want,' we were told. Not a thing that we requested did we ever get. Everything was picked by her. I used to want to write 'a new family'. I laughed as I thought of her face when she saw this, but fear kicked in and I requested a doll or a book instead.

This mischief has never left me either. I still want to write naughty stuff in reports and I taught my daughter a different version of a Hail Mary and Our Father, much to her teacher's horror.

Hail Mary, full of grace, stole an apple from Galbraiths, she bit it once, she bit it twice and gave the rest to Jesus Christ.

Our father who farted in heaven, stinky ass be thy name . . .

On Christmas morning, excited and lying awake in bed, I was scared to leave the room even to go to the bathroom and I would be hurting holding in my pee. You didn't dare move. You stayed in the room until she got up. Then you got to come down and open your presents as she ordered you to open them carefully, leave no mess. (If we reincarnate as animals, I am so going to be a camel.)

The rest of the day was spent cleaning the house and helping to prepare the dinner, and set out her 'silver cutlery' on the table. Then I would have a mountain of dishes to do after the meal, and it was a rare time someone would help. Then there was a party at night in the living room, and the drinks flowed for family members, and the children would be up the stairs. The older cousins would hang around in the BFB's room, laughing away and sneaking drink up with them.

My sister would sometimes go in and be told to get out by the BFB, but other cousins would tell her to stay in. He didn't want to look like a bigger eejit than he already was, so he said nothing. I sat in our room playing with the educational toys we had gotten, or reading a book.

Merry fucking Christmas!

I couldn't even go to bed as everyone's coats were on it. That was my job too, to take the coats off the guests and take them upstairs. We had an aunt on FF's side, and her husband worked on the oil rigs. She would come in a long fur coat and she always smelled beautiful. I remember trying her coat on and parading round the room, terrified I would get caught but giggling at the state of me, this skinny girl in a large fur. 'I'm a queen,' I would say, laughing and twirling. She would never have minded anyway. She was lovely, as was her own family. I used to relish their rare visits to this shithole. I watched Billy Connolly talking about something similar with the coats on the bed years later and I laughed my head off.

No party on your birthday. No friends over.

A table was put up in the living room and a frozen Black Forest gateau was laid out (mainly for the pictures) after dinner. No waking up to a card and a present. Going into school and trying to avoid the questions of 'What did you get for your birthday?' The card would be opened at the table and whatever shit present she decided to give would be opened then too. You did not ask for the latest fashion or the latest toy. You got what she decided. I still struggle celebrating my birthday and Christmas but do my best for my family to enjoy spoiling me. It triggers so many things. The sense of being worthy of a gift, of deserving something nice. I am working on it.

You wore the clothes she picked, you ate the food that she decided on, and you did your duty regarding the chores. You wore your hair how she wanted it and she eventually put a bowl around my hair and cut it all off with kitchen scissors. My long flowing brown hair tied in elastic like a trophy from an Indian scalping. It lay in the cabinet drawer to remind me that she had control. Of course, she told people that I had wanted a grown-up haircut and I agreed when asked whether this was true, as I had no voice. More lies from FM. She continued to cut it for me, making a bigger mess each time with her trusty kitchen scissors. No one questioned what she said. I kept my hair short till my mid-twenties because the memory of the brush pulling at my tugs and of the brush being broken on my head. Many people admired my beautiful long hair as a child and made comments. Did she hate that?

Your son liked it though, didn't he, FM? Ask him what he used to do …

Her abuse was not just for my beautiful hair. One time I fell and cut my knee badly. She scrubbed it with a nail brush to get the grit out. Because of where it was, the scab would keep bursting open as I bent my leg. I was accused of picking it. Gentian violet was then used on it, and she scrubbed again with a nail brush. Over and over she went on the raw skin. It took ages to heal and the scar is still on my knee.

I got scabies one time at school and I was put on a fold-down orange patterned sun lounger with a sheet to sleep in my room, handed my own towel and cutlery.

'Dirty girl, that's because you don't wash your hands enough,' she said. I was treated like a leper for over a week. But hey, didn't stop me doing your dishes or your washing, did it though? Still peeled the potatoes you all fucking ate every night.

Her control in everything led to further ridicule and embarrassment.

When I was a teenager and had taken my first monthly

period, FM sent FS into my room and left me a belt and a towel the size of an incontinence pad with two big loops. I was horrified. What the fuck was this?

Mrs Tampax, as we called her in school, had already showed us products for this time of the month and she missed this fucker out of her wares to show us!

My sister came to the room and had to explain that you wear the belt round your waist and loop it onto the towel. I put it on over my trousers and was walking round the room like I had shit myself. My sister was laughing her head off. I didn't know whether to laugh or cry. My sister said she would get something else from the shop. I was too embarrassed to wear this thing that had been lying in the drawer since her eldest daughter's period. A tinged grey nylon half suspender belt thingy from the seventies. I get the recycling thing, but FFS!

There were never any personal products bought for me in advance. I had to ask for 'money for thingies' – oh no, you did not dare to say the word sanitary towels in front of anyone at home. I would walk to the shop with toilet paper stuck in my pants. I would look at the shopkeeper with total embarrassment as I handed them over to pay. He would put them in a brown paper bag and offer me a sweet from the jar on the shelf. I will never forget how he tried to dampen my scarlet face. Our local shop was run by an Asian man, not that I ever saw the colour of his skin, and as I got older I would be horrified at the racist abuse he endured. He was just a kind man with a family, working long hours. I hope he was rewarded in his later years for the kindness he showed me.

If I got blood on my underwear, FM would scream that I was disgusting and that I was to wash them by hand before putting them in the washing. WTF? A time in my life when I was becoming a woman and she made it dirty and embarrassing. She forgot when I was sorting the washing the amount of skid-marks on her own family's underwear. Cheek of her!

I know the explanation of FM's behaviour time and time

again has been the main focus of the story so far, but bear with me, it will make sense in a bit. Her continued behaviours and conditioning was what enabled someone else to go on a journey that they got away with for years. She is not my issue, oh no, there was someone much worse than her, even though it looks like I am focused on her for now, but to be fair, she was a big part of this. Bigger than she can ever realise or will ever admit.

Swimming trips were fraught with panic and fear. FM would let me wear a swim vest, a padded foam thing, not like the ones now. I was terrified of the water due to her shoving my face under the bathwater or throwing a jug of it over my head to rinse my hair. She would let my brother hold on to her, not me. I clung to the sides. 'Swim,' she would order. I let go and duly went under, spluttering and swallowing the chlorine water. Grabbed roughly by the arm, I was pulled up and told to do it again. I had no trust that the water would hold me. I had no trust to relax and lie back and float. I had no fucking trust in anyone or anything.

My school uniform was so different from the other kids. No ankle socks and straight short skirts with a leather bomber. A sickly green hand-me-down parka-type jacket and long socks with T-bar proper school shoes. The school was so proud that in this deprived area, a child, who, may I add, was a model student getting 99 or 100 per cent in tests, would wear the school colours with such pride. Model pupil, job done. Her box was ticked from the school too. The shoes I had were like baby shoes, T-bar across and hard leather that blistered my ankles. In a shoe shop just before the start of term, she made me try on two pairs.

'Which ones?' she said. Both were uncomfortable and horrible. I thought that at last I was getting to pick something, as previously I had no say. Maybe now because I was going in to first year in secondary school I could pick?

'The shoes are a bit sore on my feet and the straps are tight. Can

I try on another pair please?' I said. She lifted both pairs of shoes and walked to the counter. 'We will take both pairs, please,' she said. I should have known I would never get choices or a voice.

Months later, the shoe's heel broke. I was in a total state of panic.

It was like a short block square heel. I got toilet paper and PVA glue from school and tried to glue it together as I feared her wrath. My friends gave me their chewing gum too to try and stick it together. The worst repair job in the world. I shuffled home, trying to drag the heel flat on the ground to stop it clacking and falling off. This made it worse and scuffed the broken heel.

The toilet paper sticking out the back was a dead giveaway ... I was fucked!

I stood in front of FM and FS. They were both sitting on the chairs at the side of the fire, munching away on something. They had been out shopping at the cash and carry.

'You have broken the shoe deliberately haven't you?' she said as she popped a nut in her mouth. 'They are all scraped at the heel too.'

The pee was starting to dribble again. I knew what was coming. Not just wet pants again but a punishment.

It was a broken fucking shoe. 'Not my fault you bought cheap shit,' I said in my head but dared not say it out loud for fear of reprisal. I was grounded again for being ungrateful and she made me wear old shoes that were too small and hurt my toes.

What did people see when they looked at me in this uniform and shoes she made sure I wore?

Not only was I the kid with 'two dads', I was also a 'foster kid'. No fighting was allowed in case of shame and embarrassment to the family, so if someone was bullying me or wanted a 'square go' (a fight) then I had to look like a shit-bag and refuse or take a beating. I was the kid with no tuck for playtime or no tuck money for the school shop, just a piece of fruit sometimes that she was too embarrassed to take out her bag, and that depended on what was left in the bowl each week. No tuck if someone else had eaten what was there. If the fruit ran out midweek I did without. BFB would take a banana from the bowl after his dinner – the last one – and eat it in front of us, knowing there was nothing left for me, my sister or brother to take as a snack for school.

The two dads came about because we were to call my real father 'wee da' and FF 'dad'. My sister was asked one day in school her father's name and she replied, 'My wee da or my big da?' She was laughed at in class. The teacher called her aside and demanded she explain to her what that was all about. I think she was relieved that we were not living with two gay men, to be honest. People were less comfortable about same-sex relationships in this part of Glasgow and in this timeframe.

I didn't complain, I just put my head down and worked hard to please, even when I was being ridiculed in school by kids who just did what kids do, not really knowing the circumstances behind the person. Smile and nod, Katy. Laugh it off. It was the only way I knew how to cope.

There seemed like no escape: home was horrible, and though school was a welcome break, the pressure to keep my marks at 100 per cent exhausted me. Other kids were rotten because that just the shit that kids do sometimes. Everywhere I went I was constantly scared and awaiting the next fearful situation arising.

But amongst this there were a few hidden angels: my friends. My friends that turned up with an extra treat, or they just happened to find an extra 5p in their purses for me to go to the tuck shop. My friends that took me to their houses at lunchtimes and gave me a cake – a cake at lunchtime!! A luxury! I would be dizzy with the sugar rush and sated, walking back to school after lunch with a treat in my belly.

I was allowed a slice of Black Forest gateau on my birthday. That was about it, yet FM baked for the school and for others less fortunate and gave it all to the school fete or church.

My friends in my local area played with me like normal kids, playing Dead Man's Fall off the double grass – a communal lawn. We annoyed the local caretaker of the high-rise flats with pranks, made perfume from flowers, caught bees in jars.

To any of those friends reading this, those times with you all were a welcome breath of fresh air from the constraints of that house I lived in. Thank you. Our time together was probably insignificant to you, but to me it was small touches of a normal existence creeping in. You know who you are.

My friends from school brought in clothes every day for me to change into: ankle socks and straight skirts, old jackets they had. My bag was heavy; bundled inside were the weird clothes. In my borrowed apparel, I was one of them. Even if it was for just a few hours, I was accepted because of them helping me look normal amongst the group.

My friends at home, shared their sweets, took me to their houses for a jelly peece (jam sandwich) and showed me that my reality was not normal. They invited me into their homes and helped me to understand that this shit doesn't happen in every home. I started to wake up from the haze of pain, fear, hurt and loneliness. I never told them what went on, but they could see something was wrong. They saw me kept in, peeking from my bedroom window as they played outside; they saw me stare at their sweets. I wasn't a bad kid. When I was at their house I said please and thank you. I did what I was told, polite and well behaved so that there wouldn't be any bad reports back to the FM.

My friends couldn't understand why I was always kept in. They couldn't understand when I said I couldn't go to the park on the bike. This was because the bike was in the garage and to go to the door, ring the bell, upset FM and ask for the bike to be taken out the garage was a big no. Going outside the perimeter fence of where we stayed was a big no. 'You're not allowed outside the fence.'

I hated taking the bike anyway. It had been FS's from when she was younger and was old and tatty. The other kids had got a chopper or a BMX for their birthdays or Christmas. My brother had gotten a new bike one Christmas after he had an accident and broke his leg. He barely rode it, but I was not allowed to take that.

When my friends went off to the shops or to the park on trips that I was not allowed to go on, I stayed within the fence and I played on my own, because I was damned if I was going back to that house. If I was lucky enough to be allowed out, even if I had to stand out there on my own, then it was the better option. There would be the odd 'pervert flasher' hanging around sometimes, but I ignored them – home was worse. A flasher wasn't scary compared to what I would have to endure if I went home.

I waited and watched from the sidelines as my friends came back from the park with frogspawn in jam jars, tales of stopping at the cafe for an ice cream. One friend gave me a jar with tadpoles in it and I took it home. Bad idea! I was kept in as a result because I had 'stolen animals' from a park and they were now going to die: FM flushed them down the toilet. My friends grew theirs into little frogs and took them back to the original pond.

FM did the same when at Easter all my friends had picked daffodils from the park for their mums. Hesitantly I did the same, knowing I would be in trouble. 'How dare you pick them from a public park?!' she screamed. I was fucking grounded again for trying to do what the other kids were doing for their mums, yet in my thoughts, inside my head, I wanted to lift a cowpat and leave it in her bed, not flowers.

The rules were suited to FM's changing moods.

FM's main rule for me if I was out playing was 'Don't disturb me even if you need the toilet.'

If I was playing outside in the local area near the house, I did not dare go ring the bell to go to the toilet, so I went to other people's houses or I learned to pee in the bushes when no one was looking. If I needed anything more than a pee then I had to go home, but then that was it, I was kept in afterwards. No going back. So, if you think about the statement, I made earlier about what goes in my mouth and out the other end, I suppose she did have control in a way. How dare I ring the bell twice in the one night! Imagine being scared to go home because you needed a jobby!

The bedroom my sister and I shared was like a prison cell for me. The windows were metal. In the winter, there would be ice and fungus across the bottom pane and the sill. My sister and I were sometimes allowed to put the fan heater on for ten minutes to take the chill off the room before bed. We would huddle in front of it, shivering. The breath would be visible coming out of our mouths. I'm sure one night I saw the arse of a penguin running for the door, saying he was off to find somewhere warmer.

But where were the FM and FF?

They were comfortably sitting in their chairs in front of the living room fire, of course. Their feet up on the 'pouffe', all cosy and warm.

That would have hurt the bank balance and you could not be doing without a holiday this year just to keep us fuckers warm, you did deserve it, looking after us urchins you saved! Enjoy your cruise!

As my friends became older and wiser, they sort of understood when I ran away that something was wrong and would cover for me. 'Of course, she's asked her mum if she can stay' they would say to their parents as I hid in their room, terrified the foster parents would find me if they came looking, my friends lying on my behalf, to their own parents. They lied for me, just because I was their friend and because they were children from loving family homes – not perfect, but loving. They could see right through my blank stares and quiet mouth that something was seriously wrong but were too young to know what it was and what to do about it. I never said, either.

One friend moved away to another area and I missed her so much. My friends and I all went on a bus one day to see her and I spent the whole day in a state of anxiety because I was told I was not allowed to go. I went anyway; I would take the punishment just to see her.

Another young friend died in a fire in the Easter school holiday while I was away with my FS and her partner. We returned to the news. I was so heartbroken. Her mother had previously passed and now she and her brother had died in a fire in their home. I saw her dad years later, by then with alcohol issues, and my heart broke for him.

The news was ignored by my family. I got the information from my other friends about the fire and her funeral. She was treated as just another person in my life who was now dead and not spoken about. Same old story again. No sympathy, no empathy.

None of my friends got to come into the house. My friends would have to stand at the door till my chores were done. I would peek out the kitchen window and mouth to them quietly or raise two fingers to say two more minutes. I was terrified they would stop being my friend and go call on someone else to play. They never did. They waited.

We didn't do 'sleepovers'; FM told us that 'it is a rule of social work, no sleepovers unless the parents are vetted. Do you want the embarrassment of that?'

When I was younger, I used to think to myself, 'Who the fuck was this "social work"?'

At high school, now more aware of who social work was, the embarrassment of asking my friends to have social workers come and check out their house was too much. I was not sure what a social worker was for and did not want my friends' parents to think I was a bad kid. Social work sounded like some police force. The kids I knew in school that had social workers were truanting or had problems in their home.

I would make excuses to friends about not wanting to stay over. It did me no favours. Eventually your friends find other friends and have nights in together.

There were to be no TV programmes that were deemed

unsuitable (which was mostly everything), no posters on the wall of our favourite pop star, or the new tape of the latest group. My sister and I would record the charts on a Sunday in secret, reusing the tape and standing over it so we could time when to press the pause button in between songs. That's when the plug wasn't taken off, which was FM's trick to 'show' what we had in the room without us getting any joy out of it.

I'm sure many other people 'taped' the charts, because sometimes money was tight and taping the charts on a Sunday evening was what you did, but it's not as if there was a shortage of money in this house to buy an album. It was spent on more important things, for show, not on what the children wanted for birthdays and Christmas. Social work paid a fostering allowance times three per month, yet there was never any money.

The key to living in this home was stay quiet, don't question, and don't cry too loud. Don't cough, or a pillow would be over you face for disturbing her programme. Just do as you are told.

Most of the time I did do as I was told, but sometimes I would put the TV on for five minutes when I got in from school if no one else was in yet. I would watch *Thundercats* and *The Pink Windmill*. My friends in school would be talking about their favourite TV programmes and I would stand silent, laughing when they did, pretending I knew what they were talking about. That little treat ended when my younger brother grasped that idea too, except he would not turn off after five minutes, and the back of the TV would be warm – FM would check it when she arrived home. Guess who got the slap or grounded for it. Yes, me – because I was older and should have known better and made him turn it off. Meanwhile my brother did nothing he was told to do and blamed everyone else. And FM believed him, even though he was nicknamed 'Tam Pepper'. (I had no clue who Tam Pepper was and still don't, but apparently it was someone who lied.) As much as I saw him as her favourite amongst the three of us, he still got name-called and berated.

I coughed all the time and I was sometimes sick with lots of white mucus. My younger brother was the same. But he was taken to a doctor and I was ignored. When I had to cough, I had to hold it in until I ran to a place where I could do it quietly, into a towel or a pillow from the bed so FM did not hear. I had constant itching and soreness around my private area, sore muscles, and I sometimes got so tired I felt that I would collapse. 'Don't be lying again' were her words as usual. 'Get to bed if you're sore or tired, then.' I was told I used to cry when I was small about having 'sore eggs' (sore legs) when I was younger and had to walk. They laughed at me for this too.

This ignorance from the FM and lack of caring let a long-standing hereditary immune deficiency progress to severe autoimmune issues which floored me for many years of my life. It was never recorded or acknowledged in childhood.

I had learned the hard way not to make too much noise.

One time, sitting on the sofa in the living room, I was in a coughing fit, red in the face trying to hold it in. She screamed at me to shut up. I coughed again and she erupted from her chair and dragged me up the stairs by the hair and threw me into the bedroom. I landed on the floor and got up, wheezing and trying to catch my breath as I pulled myself onto the bed. She was livid and she grabbed the pillow from the bed and pressed it over my face. As I struggled to get out from under her, she became enraged, slapping me anywhere she could with her other hand. I stopped struggling because I could not breathe.

'Stay calm, Katy,' I told myself. 'Do not move, you will make her worse.' She stopped with the pressure on the pillow as I stayed silent and still. Nothing said, she walked out of the room, the pillow still over my face. I lifted it and took a breath then, realising I had wet myself.

What was wrong with her? Why did she hate me so much?

I would find out many years later ...

CHAPTER 6

Surrounding Family

Visits and sleepovers at my dad's house were rare. FM told him he had to get permission from the social worker to have us stay over, yet when it suited her we would occasionally get to stay over at an aunt's house after a party. This was done rarely as FM did not bow to pressure. But sometimes, enough people asked her publicly and she gave in.

FM also said to my father that we could not visit when it suited her. She told him she had concerns that he was drinking again, hypocrisy raising its ugly head again. Her husband would roll in every Friday night late, remnants of a fish supper stuck between his teeth and absolutely pissed as a fart. He had also been at the doctor's and in the hospital getting treated for gout, an illness associated with drinking lots of alcohol. In the earlier days, my father would visit with his new wife, and my younger brother would be held up on FM's knee, stopped from going over to sit with him. My sister and I were upstairs in our room and allowed down to say a brief hello or sit for a while. He would stay and drink, then leave.

Sometimes my sister and I would watch from the top of the stairs to see who had visited; it was our only way of knowing sometimes of who was in the house. Other people probably thought we were rude, that we did not want to see them. Not true. We were upstairs in the prison, told to stay there until told otherwise. This was another way for FM to control who we spoke to and when. We probably looked a bit weird.

When guests visited, they were offered alcohol from FM's big display cabinet. Full it was, chinaware and alcohol, all polished and organised. My grandparents and my dad, the same people she stopped us from seeing because they were drinking, were offered alcohol and they took. I never understood her.

Christmas evening was held at this house for family, food was plentiful, and guests welcomed. None of them saw the stressed-out state FM had been in all day, taking it out on all of us. My aunts and uncles were all lovely, but visits in this family were usually limited to Christmas, hatches, matches and dispatches.

Saturday nights consisted of going down to my paternal gran's house to take her to chapel. We did not drop in for a treat or 10p. My other friends' relationships with their grannies were so different. I never really had a relationship with her at all, because FM controlled these visits too. She also tried to control her other siblings. Some put up with it, some did not. Again, as a kid I had ears. I heard what they thought of her.

Love this quote I seen recently

'I noticed everything. I just acted like I didn't.'

One of my aunts used to make tablet (a Scottish sweet, like a harder, crumblier version of fudge) at my gran's house and would usher my sister and me into the kitchen to let us lick the evaporated milk from the tin or the spoon. Make the tablet. Stir it. Taste it. Give us some to eat before FM saw us. She took us on trips to the cash and carry and she bought stuff we liked. FM never approved but had to be seen to be grateful for the gifts to us, and we wore these on visits to my gran's house. Other times it was, 'Not suitable, take them/it off'.

This happened with clothes that cousins had given us. For show only.

When I stayed over, my aunt would run me a bath to myself, filled with mango bubble bath. On one occasion, I even tried to lick it because it smelled so beautiful – not a good idea! There were scented soaps, warm towels and a clean bed with brushed cotton sheets and heavy blankets. Comforted and clean. I was in soapy heaven. She took us to fetes at a hospital over in the west end of Glasgow and we visited The Jolly Giant toy store on

Crow Road. A toy shop!!! I was like Buddy the Elf when he hears it's Christmas time!

Visits to other aunts' and uncles' houses were always a treat, and I remember every one of them fondly. It was sad that later in life I felt no choice other than to cut all of them out of my life because I trusted none of them. FM was their sister. They were all 'family', and I wanted nothing to do with them.

As a child I sadly had very little contact with my gran and grandad, my mum's parents. My gran did drink lots, she was also in bad health, and in later years she was bedbound.

One Christmas in my early years I remember my gran coming to visit at this foster home with my grandad. With her teeth in, lipstick on, powder on her face and a wool hat on her head, she looked like a different woman. They were offered drink by the FM and FF and drank. We got to see them briefly and then it was bedtime for us. I could hear them downstairs still. I cried when I heard them leaving, wanting to stay awake, hoping they would take me away with them, but I hardly knew them. What I did know was that they knew my mum. That was enough for me.

On another occasion, my older brother came with my grandad to drop Christmas gifts for us. I still didn't know him well by this point. We had been kept estranged from him all this time due to the visits being few and far between at my gran and grandad's.

My gift was a 'Charles of the Ritz' make-up set in a sparkly beaded bag. It was the most beautiful thing I had ever seen. It was promptly put away in a cupboard by FM as we were 'too young to be wearing make-up'. I did use it once and as usual I was caught out and was commanded by the FF to take it off, or he threatened to get a scouring pad and do it for me.

I craved seeing my older brother and my grandparents, but random visits to their house was all I got. My gran died when I was thirteen. She had been in the hospital, and the day before she died she was joking with my grandad that he had now got his free bus pass. 'That's you got yer free bus noo, ya old bastard,' she joked with my grandad. Crazy, mad, funny till the end.

She was cremated, and I remember being taken to this place, a small amount of people there. When I looked at my grandad's face it was drawn. He looked lost, bloodshot eyes and a blank look on his face, holding in that emotion as he did always, but nothing was explained to me except that she was dead. People died, you cried, then you never said another word about them. I was numb to it.

I was taken by FM and FS to the local Italian cafe after the ceremony finished and remember getting to pick an ice cream sundae. My younger brother and I were sitting there stuffing our faces with ice cream, unaware of the reality of a death. But that was just for bragging purposes: 'We took them for a treat.'

I felt sad about my gran, but I hardly knew her. Sometimes on a visit, I watched her lying in her bed that was now in the living room, shouting at my grandad, sometimes crying and hugging us so tight I thought she would squeeze the life from me. Her legs were thinner than my arms.

She had never gotten over the loss of my mother and drank herself stupid thereafter. Seeing me and my siblings must have reignited that pain and loss, of her daughter and her grandkids. All away. She scared me, if I am honest.

(She had her reasons: betrayal. That's on its way!)

After my gran's passing, I do not remember any more contact with my grandad. FM made sure of that.

CHAPTER 7

The Family Dynamics

The last chapter was a little about surrounding family and the 'support' I had. Not much, but they were there.

Back to the foster family now.

At the beginning of my stay with this new family, my sister and I shared a room with the two brothers – bunk beds, two small girls and two older boys.

Should that have been allowed within a new foster placement setting? Surely not? Did anyone check that?

FS had her own room. The parents had a room with the baby, my younger brother.

'Face the wall' we heard night after night, as the two brothers played with their train set with the light on much later than a child should have to endure. It was their room and they had to share. Was there an underlying hatred arising from having to share their space, their parents, and their food? Only they know the answer to that. I would still be awake as one of the brothers got into bed above me on the bunk. It was metal coils/springs that held together to make the base, no wooden slats. I remember the shape, causing a bulge in the mattress and coils.

I remember back to a moment when I was about six years old, a moment that revealed that strong sprit that I was never aware I had in me till I think back. My little feet were pressed against the coils lightly, ready to push my legs straight and bounce the BFB fucker right out of his slumber. It was so tempting, but I was too scared. Instead I imagined I had done it and laughed as he flew from the bed, awakened with shock, and landed on top of one of his trains. The images in my head were wrong for a child of six years old, but the need for survival from both foster brothers was starting to build as they had both made their contempt very clear for me.

The brothers delighted in sharing ghost stories that terrified my sister and me. We were scared to close our eyes afterwards. How they both laughed at our small faces in terror. The fear was everywhere, building and building their little enclosure of fear around me. They all had a hand in building that enclosure, every one of them.

On old 'skelp' (slap) across the head to me, or on more than one occasion to my sister, a slap to the face, marking and bruising. That came from the BFB. The whole outside family thought he was 'torn faced' (sulky) as well. Small but with ears, I heard and saw more than the adults thought I could. I listened and watched.

But to be fair there was one occasion that he did show a bit of balls. He worked part-time in a shop near the park, which my friends and I were playing at one day. I was about twelve years old. A guy dropped his trousers in front of us, and BFB must have seen this from his work next to the park. He ran towards us, vaulting over the fence, and punched the guy. I was not supposed to be away from the confines of the fence near our house, and I was terrified he was coming over to hit me.

Thanks, but maybe you should have knocked your brother out instead . . .

At some point, my sister and I unexpectedly got our own room. That was the room I described earlier, with the lock on the outside of the door.

Do you know why?

Why the FF and FM sacrificed their own room and slept on a pull-down sofa bed in the living room thereafter?

Let's see . . .

At the time, all I knew was that someone got a beating one night, screams heard throughout the house, but no mention the next day of what it was for, which was odd for a family who liked to laugh at and ridicule others and each other. No –

this one was being kept quiet . . . ssshhhhhhh, sweep. . .. sweep, under the carpet it goes. . .. sshhhhhh. Don't worry, we'll get to it in a moment.

The FS had her own room, indifferent to me because I probably pissed off her mother so often that she also got the brunt of it. She was nice enough to my sister but probably just tolerated me. But I need to say she was never nasty, never hit us. Sometimes we would have to go to her room and be given heavy books from her bookcase. I remember standing with the books above my head for thirty minutes as punishment from the FM.

Sometimes FS let us put our arms down, sometimes she watched, saying nothing as we stood with aching arms and shaking legs in the tiny space that was her room while she studied.

FM and FF called her partner a 'fairy' because it rhymed with his real name and because he was a vegetarian. She eventually married him. Wedding ensued and the only thing I have trouble forgiving her for was the blue bridesmaid dress – more frills than the Spanish doll that held the toilet roll.

The rest I can forgive as I can imagine the fear she felt about challenging any of FM's decisions. I have no issue with her or her brother (BFB). She was complacent, and he was a bully. End of. Nothing of what they ever said or did affected me in any way in my older years. I am sure their opinion of me will now differ, especially when this book appears on their lap, reconfirming everything I have ever addressed before that upset them, but I give no fucks. (READ THE RULES AT THE START.)

When the FM and FF were on a cruise on the Nile or abroad, FS and her husband sometimes took us away on holidays to a caravan with his extended family or on their own. These were the best holidays I remember having, being away from FM.

Lovely, gentle people, they were. I thought they were the most caring family I had ever seen. I will never forget their kindness to me and my sister. They called each other on the phone after visits to make sure they were home safe. FM made snide comments about this. I thought it was lovely. She was nice to their faces, of course; she played the game well.

Now we get to the important part.

CHAPTER 8

Nice Guy?

So far this is where we are at:

FF: Indifferent

FM: Hateful, controlling and violent ... the list goes on

FS: Indifferent and self-preserving.

BFB: Bully

What a lovely fucking family eh? Now we add the other brother.

PFB. Predator Foster Brother

Our main man has arrived. The party has started. Loveable rouge, always up for a laugh, funny, likeable, bit of a rebel.

The one that like to touch a child and make her carry out sexual acts, because he had to take control back, the control his mother reigned that house with.

That's what child sexual abuse is, and so is rape. It's about control.

He must have hated having to share his space in his room, share his parents, and do without because the little urchins needed. This I assume, but maybe he was just a sexual deviant, or maybe he took his feelings of rage, low self-confidence and jealousy and used them in such an abusive and calculated manipulative way ... On a child – me -for years, consistently, and getting more invasive and brutal as I got older. I was not the first, though, was I?

PFB had been caught one day by his mother doing this to another child. His father gave him a beating. That was the first sshhhhhhh we heard earlier in the story, swept away under the carpet.

This child was asked by FM: 'Why did you let him touch you there?', instantly turning it round on the innocent party.

No excuses there, FM, however you paint it. Age, family. Your son is a predator and you did nothing after this to watch him. Your golden boy, your baby. You enabled him to continue his depraved behaviour through your negligence to address what he truly was!

Was that incident reported to the social worker? Phone not working that day, exchange down, was it?

Yet there was an obligation to report it, legally and morally, an obligation for all the children in your care to be removed pending an investigation by social work and put under protection. If this had been done, further abuse would not have happened. A missed opportunity to stop this evil progressing, but you, FM, you refused to even acknowledge it, you failed in your duty of care to protect and report on numerous occasions, to save face for yourself. You and the social workers were a match made in hell.

After this event, did you not see the little girl in your home that should have been watched? Of course not, you gave no fucks, never did.

FM and FF were that arrogant that they thought PFB would stop because he got a beating. Their rules said that's it, stop it. No one would dare defy the rulers of this family, would they?

Well, he did. His depravity overwhelmed his ability to follow their rules, or even follow any moral rules.

I have a memory of him grooming me from the age of three or four years old on a holiday in Scarborough – more on that in a moment – but the first clear memory was of my communion day, where it was so vivid it stood out. A 'Holy Sacrament' white dress and cape. Aged seven.

I had fallen off a wall the day before and scraped the inside of my leg. I had a crepe bandage on it. High up my leg. I had been gifted a chain and a cross from a family member, and one of the older girls' boyfriends had pulled my cape and the chain snapped. It was an accident. I went up and showed FM what had happened. I was sent to take my dress off and change into my normal clothes as a punishment. The dress had been my sister's anyway and the cape from a cousin. It was like an itchy net curtain type of material; I was not going to miss it.

Up came PFB to the bathroom. Still wearing his black dress trousers he had worn that morning as an altar boy in chapel. 'Mum says I have to check your bandage,' he said. I never questioned this. But why make me stand at the door of my room as you looked over the top wall of the stairs? But you weren't checking the bandage, were you? You bypassed that and slipped your hands into my pants, touching me. You grabbed my hand and held it over your private area and forced me to perform a sexual act. I spend the rest of my day feeling frightened and sickened, placing a fake smile on my face while everyone was celebrating, and I did my best to avoid you for the rest of the day but everywhere I turned your face was there, playing the nice guy.

He was cunning. He stood outside my bedroom door, next to the bathroom and he sexually assaulted me. If anyone came in the front door downstairs, he would stop what he was doing and walk into the bathroom, pretending he had been in there. I was pushed back to my room, pants around my ankles. Pulling them up and glad it was over for today, a break till next time. It was relentless and sometimes occurring every day.

Remember the cloth? That cloth that everyone used to wash with in the family bathroom.

He wiped his semen on that after he forced me into a sexual act. I was called dirty for not washing. I did not care. You all walked about with his semen on you when you washed with that cloth.

I preferred to stay dirty.

My hair too, my long, beautiful hair your mother scalped from me. The hair you used to make me take out of my bobble and fall around my head as you pushed my face towards your open trousers. Was that to make you feel better about assaulting a child – pretending it was a woman?

PFB would mix up coconut flakes in water and leave it in his room in a cup to go gloopy. It resembled semen and he would ask me to try and taste it off the spoon. 'It's nice, lick it.'

Remember that, do you, BFB? He shared the room with you, so surely you saw it sitting in a cup with a teaspoon in it. Did you never think that was a weird thing to be sitting in a cup for no reason?

Wanting me to taste the semen but playing the game with the coconut paste for now. Grooming by coconut. Inventive fucker, wasn't he?

No need here to go into deep detail of the sexual assaults he undertook on me or details of the sexual acts that he forced me to perform. Fodder for some sicko to enjoy reading is not what this book is about, but I will share the facts.

I remember lying down behind that wall at the top of the stair so that he could hear the bell if my brother came to the door. My face would be next to the top of the stairs, looking down, and my legs near the bathroom door so he could jump up quickly and pretend he was at the bathroom again. I would look down at the patterns in the crazy coloured stair carpet and make patterns in my head. Sometimes I'd be lying there thinking that there was dirt on the painted edge, and I would be in trouble if I didn't get it cleaned before FM came in –anything to take my mind off what he was doing. Other times I felt as if I was leaving my body and going elsewhere.

He never wore pants and I could see an erection starting to bulge in his jeans before he sprung it out of his zip or buttons. I knew what was coming next and the pit of my stomach would flip.

He had a weird attraction to my bottom. Even when I was much younger, he patted it and would make comments – 'Look at your wee bum.'

It was continuous, wrong and against the law. He knows it. Forcing a child, from my first solid memory at seven years old, to do things you shouldn't have to do as a child.

Other memories are about the grooming and touching from the age of four years old, beginning with that holiday in

Scarborough. There were ladybirds covering the windows of the house we were in and he came to my room to take me to see them. He had me balanced on his hip. I had no pants on under my nightdress, and his pyjama top had ridden up – his bare skin on my private area. He bounced me on his hip a few times. I could feel the bone hitting me and a tickly feeling below.

He then put me on the bed and lifted my nightdress again, patting my bum with his hand. Laughing and making it seem like a game. The memories at this age are faint but they are there – and the later memories are very clear.

The sexual assaults undertaken by him went on consistently and became more invasive till I was fifteen years old. By this time, he would have been twenty-two years old. Continued to control and terrify a child. Eleven years of terror.

My rape and attempted second rape – by PFB, by then a fully adult man – happened when I was fourteen, and then fifteen. In my head, my thought process was that this was a normal occurrence, just part of the ongoing sexual abuse that was ever more invasive. For years after, I never thought or acknowledged to myself I had been raped. I couldn't.

The rape was in his brother's room. Easter holiday, time off school – perfect timing when his mother was at work and I was alone in the house, looking after my younger brother. The PFB had left home and was visiting as usual, for food or just to hang around. He led me into his brother's empty room. A brown patterned pull-down sofa bed was in there as well as the two bunk beds for my younger brother and BFB to sleep in. I complied through fear as usual. Did not question his authority.

He was agitated and flustered. He started to kiss me and asked me to kiss him back, his mouth over mine and his tongue poking in and out of my mouth. I felt sick. His breath was vile. His rubbery slobbering lips over my face and the TCP on his spots on his face made me want to gag. I turned my head away and looked up out the window and stared at the underneath of the concrete veranda on the upper floor, trying to block out what he was doing. After forcing me to perform a sexual act, he attempted to penetrate me. His words, that I will never forget, were 'You are not wet enough.'

I kept saying to him to stop, that it was sore. I tried to wiggle my hips out of the way, and I was pushing him with my arms. I was a small, skinny kid. He was over six feet tall. The energy was very different to the other assaults, and I was more scared than usual. I was panicked and kept hoping my younger brother, who was outside playing, would come home, or a neighbour would knock the door.

Pushed hard enough though, didn't you, you bastard? Did the damage, tore my skin.

I pulled up my pants and shorts and I left the room, sore and in shock. I refused to cry till I was downstairs, out of the way of him. He left the house, still agitated and flustered. I remember the white shorts I was wearing. Navy lines down the side and a tennis bat motif under the pockets. I loved those shorts. Every time I wore them after that I felt sick.

Going downstairs to do my chores, I then stood at the sink peeling potatoes. The pain was horrific. I knew my skin had been ripped and it was stinging when I had to pee, blood on my underwear, the feelings of him pushing against me still lingering. Tears were now running down my face at the shock of what he had just done. I was panicking about getting into trouble for the blood on my pants and had to remind myself to wash them before putting them in the basket.

Imagine that being your first concern after something like this happening . . . FM's control still reigned.

You could not fully insert your penis into me as a small child because it was very large, wasn't it PFB? Length and width . . .

I am sure any of your ex-girlfriends, your current wife and your ex-wife can confirm that for the record. You used to stand at the top of the stairs in your white terry towelling dressing gown, with a full erection poking out, rubbing it and beckoning me to come up the stairs. It terrified me. How would I know the size of your penis? Even if I had seen you naked, as children sometimes do in the home at bath times, it would have been flaccid. You were a grown man. You deliberately showed your erect penis at every opportunity like it was a trophy.

It was rape.

RAPE.

1 mm or 10cm of a penis forced into a vagina and its rape, no consent. My no was clear. The hurt you were causing was clear. That's the law.

Rape.

The second attempt to rape me was on holiday, but the universe stepped in.

All the years of his grooming, behaviours and assaults ended when I returned to the UK after a holiday abroad.

PFB had spent a lot of time hiding what he was and what he was doing. He would sit there sometimes and be looking at me when my siblings and I were name-called by others at home and rolling his eyes at his own parents and siblings, as if he were on our side. He knew every fear I had, watched the ridicule and used it to absolutely fuck with my head and make me feel he was the nice one of this family. It worked on a small level; I had no one else to turn to or be nice to me, so I accepted what he did and contained the shame, pain and guilt inside.

Other times when I was younger, PFB used the control that his mother reigned with. If I went to the shops with my friends and he saw me outside of the fence, he would use this. 'I won't tell mum you defied her if … ' You can imagine the rest. Being kept in or given a beating was a choice against what he asked me to do. Sick all round. Nowhere to turn; there was no lesser of two evils.

Other family members will remember you, PFB, as the funny one, the joker, easy-going. Yes, because a Hells Angel would have looked easy-going next to your bullying brother, that's why people thought of you the way you did. Nice guy. Others' dislike of your brother covered what you really were under the nice-guy tag you earned. I have a lot of respect for your brother, simply because he never covered up who he was. You, however …

You were very clever. Who would doubt you? The nice guy …

All you did was bolster the statistics of abuse within the family. No dirty old pervert in a mac here. Just a deviant, playing the game that all the deviants play. Pillar of the community, trusted scout leader, local priest, family friend, uncle, neighbour who babysat … the nice guys …

A doting father, husband and valued workmate in a position of trust that had to explain himself to them all when the police came calling. Poor PFB …

CHAPTER 9

It's All About the Money

FM took the foster money payments, times three, every month.

Here is my issue: someone was paid by the council, to physically, emotionally and verbally abuse me, leaving me in a state of fear and terror daily. It was like they were also paying her to turn a blind eye on one of her own children who was sexually assaulting me for years, the same son then used that same type of currency to keep me quiet, to manipulate me into silence because his mother withheld money.

Remember the biscuits that were stolen and replaced – how were they paid for? The biscuits that she put in the bin. Best place for them I say; they were tainted. FM did me a favour for once.

PFB gave me money from when I was around eleven or twelve years old, an odd 20p here and there when he was older and training in the medical field. I would sometimes get a pound, and on a few occasions I got five pounds and even ten pounds one time. He knew what he was doing by giving this to me. I was just a child that was happy she had a few pennies in her pocket, the same as my friends. He was the best out of a bad bunch to me, sometimes nice, sometimes snide when he would threaten to report me to his mother. I was just happy I was not being hit or ridiculed. It was that simple for me. Take what was nice and ignore the stuff that hurt.

As an adult I realised what this money was for. He was doing this to keep me quiet about what he was doing, so that he seemed like a nice guy to me. But really he was grooming me by using money as a tool because I never got any pocket money.

I spent the money he gave me on sweets, on cigarettes, on a new school skirt which my friend brought in for me each day, all the things that could be eaten or smoked. No lasting evidence of the money he gave me. To have the money on me and be called a thief was worse. For a long time and as a young adult, I felt that I was complicit in taking this money after what had happened. Shame and guilt overwhelmed me, I thought people would think I was a prostitute. Monies taken after sexual favours. Difference is I never agreed. I was coerced, forced, I was a child, I never consented, I could not consent at my age. In time, knowledge and understanding gave me clarity, and I rid myself of this issue with money.

No pocket money from elsewhere, always hungry, I bought food. PFB knew what he was doing, making himself look like the 'nice' brother. Manipulation and cunning thought led this every single time; It was not opportunistic and rare; it was calculated and constant.

CHAPTER 10

Dear FM

Yay ... holiday time ... Sun, sea and sangria. POP.

PFB joined us on a holiday abroad in an aunt's timeshare apartment ... Shit. FF, for some reason, could not come, so FM let PFB tag along.

This silver pin is excellent at bursting the bubbles around these memories that should have been lovely.

So, Dear FM,

Answer when you are ready or ignore as you always have done, but here are the questions anyway.

1. Why did you sleep in the room with my younger brother aged thirteen years old and leave me to sleep in the living area on a pull-out couch at fifteen years old with your son, a twenty-two-year-old man?
2. Why, as the two females, were we not in the bedroom, getting some privacy from the two males?
3. When you got up from your slumber and turned the light on in the apartment and saw your twenty-two-year-old son naked, holding his penis, urinating against a blow-up airbed, did you not remove me from that area?
4. Did the noise of the stream of a long-drunk man's urine flow bring you in to the living area, or did the guilt eventually hit you when you heard the scuffles and the shouting?

You told him to get back to bed after he had cleaned up his mess. He was drunk. You were more bothered about the cleanliness of the floor than the fact he was naked in front of a child. Five minutes before this, you had shouted from behind a closed door of your room, 'What's going on in there?'

Your son answered for me as his hand was over my mouth.: 'Katy is talking in her sleep.' He spoke; you believed him. I had no voice. That was the way it was.

5. Why ask that question? What did you hear?
6. Did you hear me struggle, hear me say, 'Get off me'? 'Stop it'?
7. Did you hear me try to fight him off? Scuffles of the wooden base of the pull-out couch on the tiled floor? Slaps that I made to his face and arms?

But your question *did* stop him. You then got up when you heard him pissing all over your floor.

The words you shouted stopped him from raping me for a second time – because I knew this time he was not going to stop. I knew he was drunk, and he would push further this time. I fought as well as I could this time. Fuck him, and fuck you.

I have no thanks to give you for this intervention. The damage had already been done. The sexual assaults that I'd endured long-term from him were enough to take away that gift I had to give to someone of my choosing.

Your son took that gift without my permission.

Yet you would stand at your weekly mass and preach from the pulpit, doing your readings. You'd go to the community meetings, put on your posh voice for the public, when within the walls of your own home there was terror.

You're a fake. You knew. You can deny it all you want.

You know what your son was because you caught him, and your husband beat him for it.

I laughed when I heard that your close was painted with the word 'Beast' many years ago. You thought that was me, getting at your son through you. Was that guilt that made you think that? It was someone else who did that, for someone else in the same building. All over the papers, it was; another predator who liked little girls, living upstairs. He got caught. The message was for him. The papers and no doubt everyone around your neighbourhood talking about it, yet your first thought was to ignore the reports of a clear prosecution and you think it was about your son? I never knew about it as I was not in the area. My younger brother updated me; he also told me you thought it was me. To be fair, you were lucky it wasn't me; I would have done it across your door and windows, maybe even taken an advert out on the local billboard. The difference is I never needed to. I know my truth. So do you.

It's been said after FF passed on that you were angry that for years your husband had lied to you about what he earned and left you on a tight budget while he drank, the truth of his earnings coming out after he passed away. The term should have been 'angrier'. You were mostly always angry.

I know why you hated me. You hated my father first. I was his. Simple, really. Me, the one that looked like your brother. The one that got fed different food because he could not tolerate milk when he was younger, and you did without. The one that swanned off with his new girlfriend and went drinking after his wife died, and then you were 'instructed' to take us from the children's home. Keeping up appearances for the family after you all left us abandoned in a home for over a year. You had no contact with any of us because my mum never came near you. You were not the loving aunt. My dad had been a partner and a father when it suited him, leaving her pregnant at every encounter they had in their last years together. She raised us on her own. No involvement from you. So why play the doting aunty now? You did what you were told to do because the family was being talked about in your area.

You trivialised my crying and my health, looking upon it as inconsequential or unimportant, called me 'Too sensitive', said that I blew things out of proportion. You started that false narrative of me to others early, so when later I called out your son's behaviour and your own, it looked like I was the sensitive one.

Narcissistic behaviour at its finest from you, FM ...

I left your home after this 'holiday'. I ran away, and this time they placed me in a children's home. You complained it was too near your house and wanted me moved further out as you were embarrassed. They never complied ... Your power was now gone.

You told your neighbours and family that I left your house and went into the children's home because I wanted a pair of trainers. A boy who was in a local home hung about our area. He was dressed well. You used this as an excuse to prevent others seeing what you were and what had really gone on in your house.

Let's get honest here: you hated your existence, lumbered with 'his three kids', living with a drunk and covering it up, raging that you were doing a menial job as a secretary instead of going back to teaching, something that you strived towards when your own kids were old enough. Taking us on robbed you of that.

Choices ...

You should have had more balls and said no to taking on three kids that you never wanted. Left your husband and retrained. Not taken us all on and made us pay for your unhappiness. That's why I have no sympathy for you. But the money provided by social work helped, didn't it? That paid for a timeshare apartment in Majorca that you still have, taking people there to show off, your holidays abroad. A full freezer and bulging cupboards full of food and drink, a car ... a car when no one else where we lived had one. Yet you had a pittance allowance from your husband's wage?

You may have showed others of your wealth and status in the community, but it was all for nothing.

Rather than question your behaviour when I was younger, I would cast doubt on myself and feel ungrateful because you cast yourself as the embodiment of duty and self-sacrifice. You were first-class at making me that way.

But I question you now because I would rather be battle-scarred than kiss your ass and compromise my values. You have never had any.

I'm sure you will be glad that none of your real names are being used so that no one knows who you are. I do not have to name you. You know what you are, and you know what your son is. You demanded I call you mum. You had no right. My mum will not be forgotten; you, however, will be remembered in another way by many.

It is said that people heal past trauma by forgiving others.

I have not a thing to forgive you for. You can take that to your place of worship and hope that you can muster one ounce of forgiveness to yourself for your inaction, your vicious behaviours, your abuse and your failings. Your soul's journey may be harder next time if you sit in defiance and continued denial. My forgiveness is for myself, a child who was not brave enough to speak up, a padlocked tongue with no one to listen anyway, but thank you, for making sure I was a mother that was so far at the other end of the scale, even though you tried to act like a model parent.

Goodbye, FM. You get no more of my thoughts anymore.

'Praying' – Kesha: https://youtu.be/v-Dur3uXXCQ

This is 'Katy's' story for now. The next part will cover her journey further.

Part Two

———◄◦►———

CHAPTER 11

Freedom

Iarrived at the children's home and sat through some paperwork. I was then left to sit in one of the two lounges on my own as the social worker undertook a handover with the staff. One was called the green room and the other the blue room. The blue room was for the older kids, green for the younger ones.

I was free. Free from a life I hated ... for now.

Remember that wonky-eyed tramp I had anger at for leaving me in that house after the belt? Well, I rocked up at the social work office when I was sent for the shopping on the day I returned home from that final holiday. A girl in my school had a social worker and she knew how to play the system. After hearing that I had been running away, she told me that to say I would hurt myself if they sent me back there, kill myself if I needed to. If I said that, she told me, they would have to act. I had injuries from the FM beating my head, hidden with my hair. A beating I had gotten for running away the day after PFB attempted to rape me. Again, no planning, and caught as usual.

My stomach was rumbling as all I'd had eaten all day was the social workers sandwiches.

One of the girls came in to check me out. She was the top dog, or so she thought. 'Dae ye want sumfin tae eat?' she asked.

I nodded and sat as she returned with a roll and ham, chunks of raw cabbage leaves on top instead of lettuce. I ate anyway. Did not want to look ungrateful or call her on the difference between a lettuce and a cabbage. She looked scary to me, and I wanted no drama.

I had lots of questions from the other kids: 'What you in for?', 'What did you do?'

I was confused. I had not done anything wrong. I really did not understand at that time the children's home had a mix of kids, some there due to family circumstances, some due to 'bad behaviour'. But it didn't matter. You were just one of the new kids and had to find your place in the line and move forward.

I said my foster parents and their sons were horrible. Other kids nodded in understanding. They knew this could happen. Their questions lasted all night. After that, you were just the new girl till someone else arrived.

Staff were relaxed and let you smoke. Night staff at the home were a little older and a bit stricter but with genuine concern behind it. Grandmothers and mothers themselves. I'm not so sure that qualifications in social care were high on the list in here, but it never mattered to me. The staff were decent and fair. They were caring and had families of their own.

I lay awake that first night, listening to the sounds of others in and out their rooms, staff going about their business. The adrenaline was still flowing, but I was safe. If you have ever been in a situation where you lived in constant fight-or-flight you will know what I mean. The fear never left because you trusted no one, but you took a little bit of that hope that it was going to be okay and kept it close to your chest.

The staff had given me toiletries and towels. I was clean, and no one was hurting me. Massive thing for a child. Massive.

I shared a room with two other girls to start with. Hygiene was not a strong point, but aesthetics was. If their hair was done and make-up slapped on, that was fine. I found it strange. I would languish in the shower for ages, enjoying the fact I could take one. Not a stinking bath after someone else. I sometimes had three showers a day just because I could.

I did not wear make-up. My hair was gelled back into a ponytail. Hairy eyebrows and a few teenage spots in the t zone, no clothes worth wearing so the staff arranged to take me out and get me some essentials. I was unaware of my body and did not care much for how I looked. I was just happy to be clean and out of that house. I think I was trying to wash away what I felt every time I had a shower.

I was grateful for food and company. It was bliss compared to where I had come from.

I think that was the problem. I was so glad to be here, I did nothing at first to jeopardise that in anyway. No one asked me any questions anyway. No chats about what happened or how I felt about being there. So, I said nothing. These people might send me back there. Filing the memories away in a dark space, pretending it never happened. This was my life now.

I often wonder why the right questions were never asked, nor a mental health assessment given. Would I have disclosed what had been going on? They could have given me a medical examination and see the damage too. Another missed opportunity to evaluate a distressed child and delve further. To build up a trust. To assure me I was safe and not going back. It never happened.

There was a meeting set up with my social worker and foster parents to 'repair' the broken-down relationship. Who the fuck were they trying to kid? Foster placement money had stopped … reputation damaged, that was FM's issue. FF just did not care.

I spent all day dreading seeing FM and FF. Not a chance in hell was I going back. I was prepared to run … My bag was packed.

There was a 'bungalow' across from the main building in the grounds. Staff used it for sleepovers shifts, and it was also used as a kind of transition place before you left to get your own flat. My key worker from the home took me over there.

My memory of what I had spoken out about in this meeting was blurry amongst the tears and sobbing. My adrenaline was in full flow at the idea of seeing them, but I was asked to say what was upsetting me and explain why I did not want to go back. I sat and described all the things that hurt, the punishments, the belt, the clothes she made me wear, the groundings for getting chores wrong, the constant ridicule and name-calling. The staff and social workers were a supportive presence and I felt I had said my piece. I left the most important thing out, but I trusted no one yet and I was certainly not going to say it in front of FM and FF.

FM took everything I said and listed it back to me, telling everyone how dramatic I was and that she had provided good discipline, good clothes, how dare I be so ungrateful. She had an answer for everything. No apology, no 'We care about you, let's fix this, we love you.'

She used the same story as she had for her neighbours, about me wanting to go into a children's home because I knew someone in there that had Adidas kicks, and I never. That was bullshit too. I knew of a boy from a home but I never spoke to him, and I never lusted after his trainers.

My aunt had bought my sister Adidas kicks and they were black leather with three white stripes. When they got wet, your socks went blue and so did your toes. I preferred the white leather ones with the blue stripes anyway.

My key worker from the home took me from the meeting and led me back to the home so the adults could talk.

I sat in my room thinking of ways to get out the window and thinking of where I could go to if these people sent me back there. My heart was racing, and I felt sick.

Quite soon after this, the senior social worker – the boss of my new social worker – chapped my room door. He knelt on the floor and held my hand and said, 'You don't have to go back there, its okay.'

I could have hugged this guy. I said nothing, just stared at him with tears running down my face. He will never know what he'd done that day for me. His gut instinct and awareness in his job saved me. He knew that the foster parents were controlling and uncaring. There were no investigations though. No meetings, nothing.

After I had left, the FF had got up and marched out of the meeting because he did not like what was being said. He'd been sat there, as per usual, saying nothing and ready to erupt. FM took the reins and control as usual, apparently.

Laying on my bed and relaxing into the pillow with relief, I felt like screaming with joy. But as I was accustomed to holding in my feelings I just lay there and breathed quietly.

Most of the kids from my home went to a local school but I still went back to my old school. I had funked up my uniform just a little and my friends were full of questions about the home and my new style. Along with this came some attitude, the freedom to speak my mind a little more and answer back to teachers that had been shit. I'd not quite found the right balance yet and pushed a few boundaries, because I could.

My time at my old school didn't last long and I was moved to the local school with the other kids from the home. Not a great idea. The school treated me like a delinquent and I was put in the bottom class and told to 'prove myself and work my way up'. I was a 'care kid'. In their eyes, a troubled kid from care ... It's a fucking disgrace how people throw that around. Anyone ever think to ask why they were troubled? The class was full of boys mostly who pelted the teacher and the board with soggy pieces of paper and fought in class most days. My work had not been sent on from my old school to show my marks and standard of work, so I took it upon myself to start truanting, or dogging it as we called it in Glasgow (a phrase that has a different meaning now though). As far as the school were concerned, I was just another kid from 'the home', so my education never really mattered to them. No one gave a shit. The staff at the home never pushed or talked to you about your education being important.

To pass the days, the number 89 and 90 bus did a full circle of Glasgow and you would find the upper deck full of kids doing the same as I was, or I would go down the main road and see my friends at lunchtime. On one occasion I refused to leave my room and go to school. I was lying on my bed, fully clothed and the head of the home came up. I still refused so he pulled the mattress off the bed and dragged it downstairs with me clinging onto the sides. I was then placed in the garden. 'If you don't want to go to school you can stay outside,' the head of the home shouted at me. He locked the front door. I was raging but laughing at his mischief. He was a good guy, no malice or threat in what he did. There was a meeting on that day, and heads from other homes were congregating at ours. I waved to them as they came up the drive, lying on my mattress on the grass. Within an hour I was bored and cold, so I sneaked round past the laundry room into the kitchen. The cook fed me some scones and a cup of tea, telling me she would get hung if she was caught, winking and laughing at my antics.

Preliminary exams arrived and during an exam I got up to leave because I was in the wrong one. A small man blocked my way and I shoved his arm from the door and walked out anyway. By the time I got back to the home my key worker was at the door, shaking her head. The school had called the office in the home and I had been told not to come back. The small man was the headmaster. Oops!

There went my education. No one gave a shit. No extra support. No questions asked.

There was never anything bad, but I did cause a lot of mischief and I acted out my anger. A few of the girls decided to barricade themselves in the room one day and have a fight with talcum powder. I was hanging out the window trying to breathe and laughing at the staff trying to get the door open when a big solid wardrobe was blocking their way.

The staff had lots of folders in their office where they would write some notes about you. Basic stuff, like *went to school, came in late* etc. The office had an open-door policy and you could go in and read the notes at any time. Someone had written something about me I did not like, so I left them some confetti on a few occasions ...

I had made a new group of friends and we hung around at nights together. We drank (cheaply and badly), we had boyfriends. I lost touch with my friends from my foster home not long after I went into the children's home. The last place I wanted to be was back in that area, so after a few visits I just never went back. It was nuts. I was doing all the things most teenagers do and no one stopped me. I came in on time most nights and never really caused any trouble, but I had my moments. I laughed with the other girls and boys from the home, played pranks, went out and hung around with my friends with no one on my back 24/7. I was being a teenager. It was bliss.

I smoked, drank (rarely) and even tried marijuana.

I *have a scar inside my mouth from a hash bomb that fell into my mouth the first time I tried a blowback. There I was in my room doing a handstand on the bed as my friend blew the smoke from a joint into my mouth. I did not know what the hell I was doing but we laughed our arses off anyway as we got stoned.*

I never liked the way drink or drugs made me feel – out of control, emotions surfacing that I needed to keep buried. I had to be aware at all times in case someone hurt me, so while my friends were drinking, I would pretend to do the same and act drunk, but I had been throwing mine away, bit by bit. There was an incident one time when one of the boys took advantage of a girl when she was really drunk one night. He was nicknamed after that and no one wanted to go with him when the police came to move us on. (The deal was you grabbed a boy and walked on as if you were just walking around the area with your boyfriend rather than in a group.)

Others did not understand my need to stay protected and in control.

The walk back to the children's home was over a spiral bridge or a motorway bridge. Both were pretty unsafe, and the spiral bridge was notorious for flashers. I was always on edge, always full of fear. Who was going to hurt me now?

I had started working part-time in the local social club doing silver service waitressing. I always carried a spoon and a fork in my jacket so if the police stopped me, I could say it was my work tools. But if anyone tried to grab me at the bridge, they were getting a fork in the eye. No one was going to get a chance to hurt me again.

The police used to move us on if we were hanging about and singled me out. 'Are you from the home?' they would ask. 'Yes, why'? I would reply.

'Well, get back up there and stop hanging around the streets'. There was no need to be saying that in front of the others, but I moved on. Pricks ... They were constant visitors when kids had absconded or got into trouble, so they knew my face.

I now had contact again with my dad and he had offered me a place to stay. He had split from his second wife and got a two-bedroom house, and arrangements had started for me to go and live with him. Visits ensued and the odd overnight stay was arranged. I hardly knew him or understood that he was now in recovery and attending AA, but I just wanted somebody in my family to make me feel wanted, loved. Taken care of like other kids.

As you can imagine, this arrangement went on its arse quickly. I refused to come in one night at 9pm. I said it was the weekend and the home let me out till 11pm. I was going to a disco and it wouldn't finish till 10.30. Along came the lecture of 'You will do what you are told in my house, my rules.' You can imagine my answer to that.

Why was he being like the FM? I was done with rules and duty. No one gets to fucking tell me what to do.

He contacted the home, saying I was a threat to his sobriety, coming into his house 'full of drink'. He never knew me. I was not a massive drinker. I drank a few sips and poured the rest away. I did what the other kids were doing so I wouldn't look more of a weirdo than I already felt. I was the kid from the home. No one else in my group came from a home. They had families.

I think he thought he was trying to make up for not doing his job as a father from my younger days, so fair play to him. He just wasn't ready emotionally and neither was I ready to give up my freedom and abide by the rules.

The children's home was an old house and décor was grim. Clean though. A few of us asked if we could decorate our rooms and get nice bedding. We got it. First time I had ever been able to pick my own room colours and bedding. It was grey with massive pink flowers.

I was now in a room with one girl. We hung about together for a while, but I had friends outside of the home too. It began to feel more like my home over time. You adapt. You fit in. You take what's good and you ignore the bad. You were safe, and that was the most important thing.

Now that I had some freedom, I wanted to find out more about my grandad and my mum. The head of the home found out where she was buried for me. I still have the scrap of paper with his handwriting on it.

I had got my grandad's address from my sister and went to see him every week. He would make me a milky coffee and he'd always have a pot noodle in for me, my new food of choice.

Two minutes to make and not an over-boiled potato in sight.

I broached the subject of mum with him, and where she was buried. A look of scorn swept across his face. Whenever he spoke about her, I could see the sadness and anger in him. I hated this, but I had no one else to ask. He told me she was in a 'paupers grave' because my dad had spent the money collected for her funeral. It matched the details on the tiny slip of paper that I had. It was not her name on the gravestone. It was someone else's plot, and she was in there with others.

I left my grandad's house and headed towards the graveyard. I cannot begin describing the sadness I felt when I sat on the ground and had nothing to read about who was in here. Nothing to remind anyone that she was there, nothing but the slip of paper in my hand confirming the plot. The owner of the plot had his headstone. I walked to the nearest hardware shop and I bought a frame with a poem on it.

'What is a Mother?' was the heading.

It was cheap but I marched straight back down to the graveyard and I dug a little line with my fingers and pressed the bamboo frame into the ground.

'There you go, Mum,' I said. Pathetic-looking two-pound frame and picture, but she was acknowledged.

I sat sobbing. Anger welling up by this point amongst the tears, my nails dirty, trousers all wet from the muddy grass.

My anger was about the grave but also because I never knew who she was, I never remembered anything about being with her. I felt like a fraud, grieving for someone I could not even remember, but I knew she was a part of me and the reason I existed. More anger bubbled up at the belief that my father had left me to the system and the abuse from his own blood sister and her son.

I left and went back to the home to shower and change. My friend was going with her boyfriend to his mum's partner's nightclub. He had the keys and declared it was free drink for all. It was around 3 o clock in the afternoon. We danced and drank. The three of us in this club, what a sight. We drank to excess. Being a lightweight, I was out my head. Don't ask me how I got on a Glasgow subway train and ended up at my father's door, but I did.

My venom spewed from me before he even had a chance to ask me in. I'm sure I made a few threats and called him every name under the sun before he told me to 'fuck off'. He was getting sober and did not need this. Standing in the street outside his house, I looked for a brick or a large stone to smash his windows with. 'Ya wee bastard!' I shouted as he hovered behind the curtains.

As I staggered along the road, drunk and upset, I realised I had company. The old boys in blue decided to ask me into their warm car for a chat.

It was the usual good-cop-bad-cop routine. I vented, slurring my words. The bad cop got called a few choice names. They dropped me off at the home and I headed for my room. I woke up about four hours later. The bed was overturned and the room was wrecked. I'd gotten my anger out, it seemed . . .

What's that saying? 'Gin makes you sin.' Never drank it again after that.

The staff at the home were sympathetic when I told them why I had got drunk and what I did. I was a little bit scared about the repercussions, but there was no punishment, just a listening ear, a cigarette and a hot cup of tea. But again, no questions about why I was angry and upset.

This new freedom of slowly learning to express myself verbally and physically was cathartic. It set the standard of how I continued in my life doing the same. Consequences came from that, but I have never been one to not call a spade a spade.

I hate lies. I'd rather lose what I am telling the truth about than kiss people's arses and keep what's at stake. People, jobs, the list goes on.

My headstone will say: I followed no one and learned from everyone.

Anyway, life went on in the home. There was no abuse. No beatings from staff. I know others were not so fortunate in other places, but this home was safe and fair. I cannot express this hard enough. I was lucky I had no other shit to deal with after leaving the foster placement.

The cleaning and kitchen staff at the home were also just as supportive. One of them – Belle – had a son my age and she took time to help me with my washing and my appearance. She was a gem. She would keep an eye on my washing in case any of the others stole it.

I *used to wonder how my size 6 pants ever got around their fatter arses. 'Thieving bastards, knicker knockers,' I would mutter as I took my half-empty basket back up to my room.*

I was living my life, doing what my friends did … but I was deeply naïve about people, relationships, sex. I blagged my way through conversations, pretending I knew what they were talking about. Some of the girls were sexually active and I asked one time, 'Does a boy have to pee in you to have sex?' This resulted in puzzled faces from them, and a hysterical uproar of laughter was my answer. Boy, did I feel like a right eejit.

My face red with embarrassment ...

The words echoed in my head from PFB: 'You're not wet enough.'
I thought someone had to pee to be wet ...

One day I was in the shower and I was itching between my legs.
I rubbed the cloth between my legs back and forth, but my skin was
raw, and it stung worse.

'Dirty bastards,' I screamed as I marched down the stairs in my
towel to the office.

Upon opening the door to a staff meeting I again shouted,
'Dirty bastards have given me the gonorrhoea, they have been
sitting on my fucking bed and knocking my knickers again'.

I had heard conversations about catching gonorrhoea amongst
certain people within the home

Dripping wet and with a red raging face, I was led out of the
office to a stifle of giggles from the staff.

My key worker explained how you contract an STI. She asked if
I was having sex. Horrified, I said, 'No way.' It sunk in after a
longer chat. Fuck. This was going to cause a few fights for me. I had
blamed them. I had thrush. Not 'the GHONNORHEA'.

A visit to the doctor and an in-depth sexual health lesson
occurred straight after. I was shocked when nobody caused a fight
when I got back to the home, the way it would usually go if
someone had spilled a secret. I think this is because no one wanted
to shout the word 'gonorrhoea'.

The visit to the doctor's was the first of many. Stomach issues
were also a major thing for me as well as the constant infections.
I was diagnosed with IBS. Later, we see what had been really
going on with my health.

There were always fights going on, mostly due to thieving of
others' stuff. But one of the boys would take it a bit far
sometimes. I was walking up the stairs in my housecoat
(dressing gown). Me, all sassy with my high-heeled fluffy
slippers on. One of the older boys tried to lift my housecoat.
The fluffy slipper found his head. As he came up to retaliate, I

had a bar of imperial leather soap in my pocket. It had just been picked up from the office. Smack! I swung the housecoat and the soap caught him right on the face. He never bothered me again. Not great for him, but taking the power back and defending myself was good for me. He was chancing his arm for a look or a grope. I was learning to say no and to fight back. It felt good to say no.

The staff gave out the toiletries, which were stored in the attic. You asked as you needed them and were never restricted to an amount. I had the smoothest legs in Glasgow and enough monthly sanitary products stacked in my drawer to save me from any embarrassment I used to have over this.

My issue was Stock, Aitken and Waterman. Not the kids or the staff.

One of the girls who was new to the home had her own room and she had learning difficulties. She played every one of their artists day and night and sang along. I let rip late one night as I had work in the morning, so I went into her room and ripped the cord from her cassette player and threw it down the stairs. I felt like a cruel bitch, but it was like part of family life. You fought with your brothers and sisters at home in a normal situation. That's what we did in there too. Nobody was beaten up. We just squabbled and annoyed each other when we got pissed off.

On another occasion I awoke one night to noises in my room. All I could see was a bare arse going up and down on the bed across from me. I thought, 'Why is she in bed with no pants on tossing and turning?' I turned over and went to sleep. Not a clue I had.

Found out the next morning it was not her arse. It was someone else's!!

Most of the girls were on the pill and I soon joined them. I had a boyfriend and thought it was the right thing to do as they were all 'doing it', having sex.

It was a train-wreck. It was New Year's Eve in my cousin's

house. My boyfriend and I were babysitting and we tried to have sex. I told my friends when they asked that we had 'done it and it was great', but I knew it hadn't happened properly. It had only happened the one time and of course we split up not long after. When I did eventually have sex, it was with a boyfriend that was a bit older. It was normal teenage sex. Nothing mind-blowing. I never really let myself go. This was the case for years after. I just never got the 'big wow' that everyone was talking about. I was so disconnected from pleasure and my body because of what had happened in my earlier years.

Like many other teenagers, sex was a bit overplayed. You don't realise this until you are older and in a loving relationship with trust, clear boundaries and friendship all thrown in the mix. My childhood would affect me in many ways to come for years without me realising it, but sex was the biggest issue for me for a long time. But hey . . . fuck you, PFB. I won that battle too eventually.

My education was short-lived and now that I was sixteen and had a YTS (Youth Training Scheme) job, I was transitioning from the home over to the on-site bungalow to prepare myself for living independently. It was a joke. All the kids would spend the budget on the basics and the rest on whatever we chose. We knew the cook would always feed us anyway. Nothing like real life. My friends enjoyed visiting though; they came to 'Katy's kitchen' for food and we hung about in there when the weather was bad.

There had been little contact with any of the foster family. FM visited to drop off my clothes not long after I was settled there. The bag was full of the 'Sunday best'. All the stuff I wore to family occasions and chapel where she wanted to make an impression. None of my books, no certificates or trophies that were mine. I had earned them all and she was still displaying them in her home as a reminder of how clever she had helped me to become.

My grandad's mother, my great gran, who he now cared for, had passed away. FM came to the home to notify me and she hugged me. I stood in the large hall of the children's home in total shock.

A hug.

A fucking hug. I stood in her embrace and kept my hands by my side. The staff stood by and watched.

FM was good at this shit. Still trying to keep her true self covered and play the game of the doting foster mother that still cared for this kid even after all that she had put her through ...

'Breakaway' – Kelly Clarkson: https://youtu.be/c-3vPxKdj6o

CHAPTER 12

My First Angel

When I left the home, I went into what's called supported accommodation, a flat that was furnished for you with the essential things, and I got it for one year as a start. After that, I was on my own. It was as simple as that. From the home to out on your arse. Help for a year then on your own again by the time you were eighteen.

This bit confused me at the time. I thought they did this for everyone till they were eighteen. Not so. I found out later in life why I got 'help' till I was eighteen.

Most kids from 'normal' families are either still in education or working for their own money to enjoy life.

No further education. No support. Get a job because you are going to need the money to pay for the roof over your head and feed yourself. The staff were happy to see you move on and promised to visit, but they had younger kids to look after now. Most of the teenagers around the time I was there had moved out, and the home was filling up with much younger children, sadly.

There were a few visits and calls, and then it dwindled. On paper, I was one of the better-behaved ones. I would do okay.

I was encouraged to build a relationship again with my family when I left while I was now staying in my flat. FM visited and brought me a set of pictures for my wall. Her daughter and son got a washing machine as their house-warming gift; I got three pictures of vases in shades of pink and grey.

Still playing that game ... reminding me of the difference between her own and me. I had no worth and deserved nothing but a small crumb of a gift for my new home.

I had a key worker for this flat, and she visited to make sure I was looking after myself and paying the bills. We went for lunch. I ate lots. We went for coffee. I ordered cake. I got my head down and worked an extra job at night cutting onions the size of melons in a kebab shop and mixing the pakora. My friends would be hanging around outside the shop on the streets or would pop in for some food. I stank but I got fed, so I never complained. I would fall into bed exhausted and get up the next day to do it all again. But hey, I was winning at this independent shit. My meals at home were from a tin but I was never starving. I had a phone installed, which was a luxury, and bills to be paid so the food was last on the list as a priority. I would eat gratefully whenever it was offered.

I left my YTS and decided to do hairdressing. This was when I met my oldest daughter's dad, in the pub next door to where I worked.

Likeable, cocky young guy … you know the ones … Along came my first wee angel. I was eighteen. On my own.

As you can imagine, it must have been a shock and a big responsibility to him so I would never feel the need to say anything bad about him in here, but one time something he said struck me to the core. He shouted the words 'You were not even a virgin when you slept with _____. You're a cow.' He was talking about the boy I had been dating before him. How could I explain that I was never given the chance to be a virgin to start with … ?

This was the first time that I had had a clear thought about what had happened to me. The other time had been when I questioned the girls about a boy peeing in you to have sex, but I had shut that away.

Thinking of how horrible my life had been was not an option at present, nor would it be for some time. I was looking forward to happy times with my new arrival. Maybe I looked for comfort in a partner too quickly, had sex when I should have waited. I never knew the rules of dating, or relationships or of people in general. If someone was nice to me that was enough for me …

looking back, it's so sad. Sad that I was still craving love from anyone that offered their time. I felt worthless, felt grateful to just have someone, even if it was not the right someone for me.

I'm sure the psychologists can explain this better than I can, but it's like the need for approval, to be loved and cared for, are ingrained in a child's DNA and if missed then the attachments that follow this experience can be negative.

If I thought the responsibility of running a house and looking after myself was challenging, then this would be too. But I never wanted to appear weak, so I never asked for help or complained. Still naïve. I was a small child in a woman's body playing at being an adult. But no one could ever say I never loved and cared for my daughter. She was my life, still is.

I felt worthless and tainted for so long, but this little perfect bundle started to fill the cracks in my heart and hasn't stopped since. To my best friend ... my wee favourite ... (Don't tell your sister or your brother) x

'Fucking Perfect' – Pink: https://youtu.be/ocDlOD1Hw9k

CHAPTER 13

Butterfly Returns to the Net

I was a seventeen-year-old kid, pregnant, looking for support, trying to act like an adult now. I was going to be a mother. I needed a 'family' to help, apparently.

FM stepped in and took control, again. She told me my daughter had to be christened. I had run away from what controlled me and pretended I was okay. I never dealt with it. My brain buried it and I stepped back into the shit reality of an existence that was toxic. I smiled and said nothing, as I had always done. I was back to doing what I was told. The cycle had not been broken ... yet.

PFB, you still played the nice guy, didn't you?

He would be 'brotherly' and drop by in his car outside my home with his wife, beeping the horn, offering a lift to FM's house for a Sunday dinner.

He slagged her off, still in grooming mode. He said, 'At least we get fed.' He was hungry too, never had any money for shopping.

I had repaired the relationship with my dad again and he was now back with his wife and family. They were supportive in my pregnancy and they bought lots of essentials for the baby. Feeling like a failure and a disgrace being pregnant and not with the father, my self-esteem and self-worth were at an all-time low, so I went back to visit the foster family. I did what others thought I should do and got on with it.

Maybe now I was an adult with a child of my own, I would be treated differently.

No chance. I was never free. I just got the chance to spread my wings as a butterfly from the cocoon for a little while, and I was now caught back in the net of their conditioning. I was still scared of their judgements, their opinions. I believed I had to be seen to be part of the family and conform.

My daughter was christened, given a family gown to wear, which had been brought back from Spain and worn by the other grandchildren. The party followed afterwards in my home, where they all ate and drank.

I did not even go to chapel but there I was, doing what I was told ... again. There are pictures of my grandad that day, and you can see the contempt on his face at having to be around these people again. He got drunk. The foster family didn't stay for long. FF took his pictures as usual. The camera was always at the ready ... staged for the albums.

I felt like a failure and a fraud. I had no need to have her christened. I was never going to go near a chapel again. God had no place in my life, but I came from a family that went to chapel. It had to be seen that I was doing the same.

I did my duty – visits to the foster family – mostly on a Sunday because that was when her own children visited. Sunday roast on the table. FF took videos of my little one, and pictures. He would slip me an odd fiver going out the door and say, 'Get some fags.'

He gave me pictures of me as a child. Until then, I'd had none. FM had given me nothing personal when I left but my clothes. FF was never shitty with me at this point. He was just a man that maybe understood what it was like to put up with FM's control and moods. Unfortunately, the real reason for my leaving was still never brought up. Sometimes I wish I had told him, because I'm sure he would have beaten the shit out of his son for what he had done.

I was only tolerated, and I knew it. Not only had I brought shame on this family by going into a children's home, but I was now pregnant, with no father around for the child (which wasn't true – we were just not together; his family have always been there for my daughter).

I had already thrown their generous care for years in their face by going into a children's home, and now they were vindicated as I had come back, needing them at last.

BFB would step over my daughter lying in her bouncer and ignore her, a baby – that gives the measure of the man he was. He would ask who wanted a coffee and ignore me when I said I did. I never wanted the coffee, but I just wanted everyone to see that I would never get one anyway. FS was full of patronising advice as she was now a mother too, but she was harmless really.

PFB was married with a son, and his wife was a bit quirky. Pale make-up, backcombed hair and rock-chick type of clothes. I loved her. We got on well as we knew we were the outsiders, plus she was so easy-going. A good soul, quietly spoken. I had watched this family treat her like they had treated the FS's husband years before; nothing had changed.

FM and FF would walk by my house on a summer's evening to visit PFB and FS, who stayed along from me, and pick up their kids to take to the park. Not once did my door chap. The line was still clear between 'her own' and 'his three'.

It left me feeling like the cuckoo in the nest again. But I took what was good and ignored the bad stuff. It became as easy as breathing. You're a kid, you want to be loved. You want a family. It's sad when I look back and realise what a position I had put myself in, but it wouldn't be the last time I did this. I craved love. I chased it for years.

I look back from the position I am in now and find it hard to explain to people why I went back to them. They find it hard to believe that this strong, say-it-how-it-is, take-no-bullshit woman could be that vulnerable and weak. Still groomed and conditioned.

But they say there's a reason for most things. And there was.

Oh, poor PFB, it was shameful you had to go there to eat because you had no money for your family. Was that the universe paying you back just a little?

You pretended to care. When I was at college and needed a placement, you offered your expertise as a psychiatric nurse. You worked with vulnerable people. You got me a placement at your place of work one day a week for experience on my course.

I heard you when you vilified patients, naming some of the people that were in there as being part of the 'Glasgow underworld'. That was confidential. Even I knew that was a no-no in my training on confidentiality, but you used it to brag about your job and how these people were scum.

You were still playing the nice guy, but I saw you more and more for what you were – small bits, but enough. Trying to make up for what you did to me or making sure you kept up the pretence of being a nice guy, making sure no memory would arise of you being a bad guy, still manipulating the surroundings. Watching for me to say something, how scared were you then? Shitting yourself, I bet. Hoping I wouldn't remember?

Your wife was treated like the other additions to the family: name-called behind her back. She eventually left you. She came to me to help with your son's, to watch them for half an hour until it was time for nursery while she worked. I did that for her, not for you. I had no issue with her; she was treated like crap by your family and I empathised with her.

One day I looked at my daughter, as a mother does, and I decided again that the toxic environment that your family existed in was not what I wanted for her. I stopped visiting. Your mother's Sunday dinner was not that good that I would put my daughter in this position for food. I kept in touch with your ex-wife and one time I was at a party at her house. Someone said, 'Is her ex your brother?' I said, 'Yes,' and she replied, 'Nice guy.'

Boom!!!!

My head said, 'Is he fuck.'

That's all it took: a stranger's words and all that hard work you did to cover it was blown in your ex-wife's parents' house by a simple statement. Not blown open to where it is now, but a crack. Remember that every time you see her or look at your sons' faces. In the house they were living in ...

Those words brought me slowly out of the blur and the burial of

what you are and brought many memories to the surface for me –
a small burst, but enough to open my mouth. Over the years I
exhumed the memories from the locked drawers and made sure
they were kept on the table ... for when they were to be reported.

I left your ex-wife's house and travelled home. Over the next
few days I remembered bits and pieces. Memories seeping through
to my present existence – and I was a mess.

I disclosed some of what had happened to my father and my
sister. My memory was quickly burying them again faster than
ever as I felt the physical pain, I smelled your TCP that you used to
put on your spots on your face.

My dad came to my house. He listened but barely acted. Not a
hint of a query, not a question. Probably shocked and numb. He
called your mother and told her what you had done, and she
denied it for you.

Did he only ring FM because he had spent years being berated
by her as an awful father and this was his payback? Blaming her
for fucking up with his daughter, so he could release some of his
own guilt? Perfect sister had fucked up and he got to feel a little
better that he was not the only fuck-up in the family. My dad was
going to see some dodgy friends and get a gun. You were going to be
shot for what you did. He didn't care about the consequences. You
were lucky. Someone smart talked him out of it.

But she did question you PFB, didn't she? There was a family
meeting.

Concerns were by now being voiced by others about certain
memories that a person had. 'Why was his motorbike outside the
house, yet you or he did not answer the door?' Motorbike ... You
were an adult.

FM discussed it within the family, her family, no one else.
Sweep, sweep went that old brush again. Under the carpet it went,
and you sat while your mother called me a liar and a dramatic
child. No mention of the time that she had caught you before I bet.
Ssshhhhhhhh, but you all knew it had happened before, surely;
you were all old enough to understand what the beating was for?

You called me at my house on the phone about a week later, after my father had called your mother and you said you were sorry – though you did not specify what you were sorry for. You asked to come and speak to me and you kept saying you were sorry. I told you to fuck off and that I was calling my dad, and I hung up. That was the last time you got to speak to me, or me to you.

Did you tell your mother and father that? Or your brother and sister? That you apologised and wanted to speak to sort 'it'. Bet you didn't. I should have taped the call on the answer machine tape and kept it. Hindsight is a wonderful thing.

I called your ex-wife and told her what you were, what you had done to me. My concern was that you would be doing the same to your sons – and now a daughter with another partner. Sexual abuse has no gender. Power and control.

Her words were 'It's hard for me to believe he could do that, he was my husband, but I do not believe that you are lying.'

Words from someone who hardly knew me. Knew me enough to trust me with her son's and she saw the treatment of me by your mother and your family. I had been on holiday with her. She knew I said it as it was, no lies. End of. I left her to make her own decision on it and never contacted her again. I felt sick that I had to hurt her with the truth.

Your lie.

Your sexual assaults on a child. Your rape of a child.

See that personality that wanted to fight back as a six-year-old kid under your brother's bunk bed? The one that wanted the truth out ...

It was ignored by you and your family; the police had no interest the first time ...

Well 'Surprise Surprise', shouted loudly in the local dialect you hear daily in the place you ran to, shouting in your ears, reminding you this is never going away. You have had years to take me to court civilly for slander? Instead you ran, you hid, you slandered me alongside your mother and called me a liar. You thought it was all over and no one would remember. Slowly you were trying to pretend you had a life and you were the victim in all of this. No luck...

Someone quite recently asked me, 'Why did you babysit for him if he'd done that you'?

Good question, thanks for asking ... even though it had an underlying tone suggesting that I was a liar. Well, I never babysat for *him*; I helped his wife out with their son's, not him. I had nothing against her.

But yes, I was in his company at his mother's house. I would go in the car with him and his wife to his mother's house. I was at university studying in the medical field and his mother said he should get me a placement at his work. I took it – still conditioned and doing as I was told.

I cannot explain this. I wish I could. As worthless as they made me feel, I felt obliged to visit, to be part of their family. I thought I owed them. Owed them for the years of 'care' I had been given.

A strange familial fucked-up attachment is the only way I can even try to explain it. Feel free to ask a psychiatrist!

If anyone has been in a similar situation to mine where a family member does this to you, you might understand this. As a strong person now, looking back I berate myself sometimes for not addressing it sooner, for not challenging him face to face, for being in his company.

This is the hard part to say.

PFB was not a bad guy outwardly; he was the joker of the family, not snide to me or my siblings. Never gave me a beating. He had been the only nice person to me in that house for years, and yes, he had an agenda behind it.

He used this to abuse and manipulate me for his own sexual gratification. That's the bad part of him. He was a manipulator and a groomer. He was doing what he had to do to keep his cover from being blown, still being helpful to me in front of others. Most abusers will be very similar. He, like his mother, was good at what he needed to do in the public eye, and behind closed doors it was a different game altogether, two faces.

I never went near any of the foster family or my extended family again. I knew, he knew, and his mother knew what he was. Fuck them. There are always casualties in a war and many other family members who had done nothing to me were out of my life. It was like they were guilty by association, by being related to FM. Was that fair to others? Probably not, but many chose their corner, or stayed on the fence and said nothing about it. Others did and were vilified as being as mental as I was. Not my circus, not my monkeys!

It was just how I dealt with it. I walked away and cut people off.

I had a few weeks off from university when this was disclosed and then later in a practical exam, one of the lecturers placed a cup of TCP antiseptic next to me because the patient's feet were smelling a little ripe. Shaking and nearly slicing this man's feet, I finished and left. Hospitals triggered me because it where PFB had worked, the smell on his work-clothes and the TCP made me feel physically sick. My career was over. I was going to find something else to do … again. I left. I was bringing this out, processing it, trying to understand it.

It was the start of a very long journey.

I did call the police and ask for advice on what to do. Brushed off was an understatement. 'It happened a long time ago. Are your memories clear? You will be grilled in court.' At that point I'd been too scared to report it, and not all my memories were coming out, so I put down the phone. I had been about to open a can of worms and I truly wasn't ready. I guess it was not the right time.

'The Voice Within' – Christina Aguilera:
https://youtu.be/nA2k79EGHbc

CHAPTER 14

Moving Forwards

That little breakthrough of disclosure did help a little to release my fears and help me start to grow.

I was a bit more vocal, a bit stronger. I faced more things, but I was never settled – in my job, my home or my relationships over the years that followed.

People are people, me included, and people change. Sometimes the love from friendships and relationships was good, and sometimes it was not. Simple as that. I learned what I wanted from people and learned what I would not put up with, as I am sure they did with me. I do my best to own my behaviour as an adult and it's been far from perfect or 'normal' in many situations; I fully recognise that.

I remember seeing a picture of a Guardian Angel with her head in her hands and I thought, I bet that's mine.

So, if you are in my life, there is a good reason for that. If you are not, that's just how it is.

Years of friendships and relationships, be it work or personal, have shaped my experience and it's all good. I tend to walk away and cut everything, ties, feelings and any contact. Disengage. It's easier than hurting.

I explained earlier about being at university.

I was a smart kid and I decided I wanted to return to education, so I did. School was fucked due to living in a children's home and being a 'care kid', so here was my chance.

I probably drove some of my lecturers mad with my constant questions because I needed to know clearly what I was learning. I had no time to go home and study. I needed to work and be a mum too. One said to me one day, 'Don't worry, you're just asking the questions others are too scared to ask.'

Still do. Always will.

Sadly, the career paths I kept trying to take were affected in some way almost all the time with my triggers from my past. So, jack of all trades and master at none will just have to go on my CV.

There was a lot of moving homes, a lot of changing jobs, but nothing juicy. I got on with my life mostly away from Glasgow but if I'm being honest, it was an existence. Never really living it but existing for the moment. Challenges came up, good times, not so good times. Same for most people, really.

I kept my past in the past, where it was one of my main background noises I ignored. I did not want to be known as the care kid, the abused kid, the raped kid, the fucked-up kid. Sometimes it reared its ugly head, not enough for me to address it properly but enough to remind me it was there.

People have said to me, 'You are running from your past by moving away.' There is maybe a bit of truth in that. But no one knows when you are strong enough to stop and face the monsters of your past…no one should judge when is right.

'Runnin' (Lose It All)' – Naughty Boy ft. Beyoncé, Arrow Benjamin: https://youtu.be/eJSik6ejkr0

CHAPTER 15

Business

Learning quick and bordering on perfection at most things I do because of fear of failure led me to realise that others were benefitting from my skills, so I decided to start my own business.

It was aromatherapy-based and I started in an era where education was key to my product. It's different nowadays where 'alternative' products are within mainstream everyday products, like lavender fabric conditioner etc. Back then it was almost airy-fairy and I should have maybe been the stereotypical sandal-wearing hippy. But I was smart-suited and smart-mouthed, always feeling the need to be different or succeed, but in reality felt I was really broken and different from my peers.

I was ahead of my time and deeply naïve about business, but I went in guns blazing anyway. Some press followed and after all my hard work I lost the exclusive sole rights for distribution to import my product from America to Britain to a company that saw an opportunity and used it. Simple.

I was a small sole trader and they were a limited company. Fucking wide-os (Glaswegian slang for fly guys).

The director had the balls to call me after and asked for me to go and train his staff. Let's just say I left him blushing. (You can't beat an angry Glaswegian woman in a rant.)

Not sure if it's a Glaswegian thing or general thing, but I remember hearing shit like 'Oh, you won't want to know us when you're rich and famous', 'You're moving to where? Is this place not good enough for you anymore?'

Then when I no longer had my business, it was a case of 'I knew it wasn't going to succeed anyway.'

It never ever mattered what people's opinions were going to be because underneath this façade I had built, I never thought I was worthy enough to shine my light anyway.

If you want to try and be a better version of yourself, educate yourself, have a nicer home and life for you and your kids then so what? Just because you come from a housing scheme* or an under privileged background does not mean that you can't have dreams and courage.

'Do My Thing' – Estelle, feat. Janelle Monáe:
https://youtu.be/TDVMnQGqIXU

CHAPTER 16

My Second Angel

I'm standing naked in a room, bright lights and a blank canvas behind me.

I'm pregnant and I am due my baby in two weeks' time and laughing my head off as the photographer is asking me if I needed to cover up between sessions and offering me a terry towelling dressing gown. The same white terry towelling dressing gown that PFB used to wear. No thanks mate, no terry towelling gowns for me. To be honest all I could think of right then was how my bikini line looked as I could hardly see under my belly.

It was a pregnancy shoot, clothes on and clothes off. The newspaper used all the naked ones of course.

It was a celebration … of being a woman … of my body doing what it was best at doing. It was public and it was going to be seen and read by thousands. But my agenda was deeper than me just doing the shoot …

It was a great big 'Fuck you, you never won!'

I was loved. I was starting to heal a little. I wasn't as broken as I thought, and I hadn't gone on a path of pure self-destruction or been a drunk, on drugs, or god knows what. Many do not get that luck. Circumstances and issues arise from you dealing with the past, and that path can be so easily followed. My choices never took me down that path. I was luckier than many.

So, when I heard the comments, the gasps of 'Oh my god, you were naked', it never bothered me one bit. My partner, my daughter and my grandad had all seen the proofs before it went to print. They were proud and so was I. That's all that mattered.

It upset many, but I'm used to upsetting people and taking them out of their box with my words or actions. It's who I am. That will never change. She's a blessing, like my first angel and I am extremely proud, still to this day, of them both equally.

For my wee favourite. (Don't tell your sister or brother!)

'Not Even the King' – Alicia Keys:
https://youtu.be/ahsFa6AYRaQ

CHAPTER 17

Goodbye, Johnnyfartpants

Out of all the parts in this book I have had to draw from the files I prefer to keep in the 'do not open' drawer, this chapter must be the hardest for me to write.

I'm using his nickname, which my eldest daughter gave him because he always used to make loud rifting (burping) noises and she'd laugh her head off every time.

My grandad. My mum's dad.

My best friend and my source of constant support from when I was sixteen years old until I was thirty-four.

He gave guidance, he made the best soup, he never judged. He was my constant ray of sunshine.

My kids adored him, and he was a constant in their lives too. They loved him as much as I did, if not more.

I spoke of him earlier in another chapter. I had little contact with him when I was younger and made sure I found him when I went into the home in my teenage years. Visiting him and getting to know him was a little daunting at first. He was sad, he was bitter about losing his only daughter. He had looked after his wife till she died, and he looked after his mother till she died too.

We used to laugh at my great granny complaining that he must have been drinking the Baileys and eating her cake because it was nearly finished. She would get up during the night and cut herself a wee bit of cake and pour a glass of Baileys, and the empty glass in the kitchen worktop alongside the crumbs and the knife where a dead giveaway in the morning.

She was ninety-two. Still full of mischief . . . I liked her style

Around the time I was pregnant with my daughter, after my great-granny had passed, he had to move out of the flat because the tenancy was in her name, and I wondered if he would disappear from my life again. He stayed with friends in an old area from earlier days until he got his own home again – thank god, or I might have had no one that truly cared about me.

He had shown me how to decorate, to paint and wallpaper. We decorated his house together, as we had done in my house. He had his own home, his own space.

You know how you feel when you are sitting on a trendy sofa with smart décor in your own home, but there's nothing better than going to a place of comfort. A flowery sofa, shocking cushions, a pot of home-made soup, wool blankets on the bed, two bars on the fire and a view over Glasgow that stretched for miles. Heating on so full that you could grow tomatoes easily, but that was the only thing that was wrong about that picture. No needle to pop this. It was real. It was the best. It was his décor, his space, and it felt like mine too.

I would slurp my soup with a chunk of crusty bread and lie on the sofa, safe in the knowledge my daughter was being sung to, played with, educated, but most of all loved. I watched her, in awe of him. She'd be gazing up as she sat cuddled in his arms on his chair. It was my comfort.

For a long time, he had no teeth.

'Grandad gums' my daughter called him.

I will never forget when he got a new set of dentures. He visited my house every Thursday and my daughter and I would watch for him walking over the small hill near our house, bunnet (flat cap) on his head, and a bag full of goodies. Soup in a dish and strawberry tarts in a box as usual, his treats to us.

He walked into my living room and I was shocked. It was like looking at Shergar the horse.

I was laughing and crying at the same time and my daughter was hiding behind me. The teeth were hilarious but it changed his whole face and it was freaking me out. We stood laughing and looking at each other for ages. He thought it was hilarious the state I was getting into. It looked as if he was constantly smiling, this gleaming set of fucking enormous teeth. He still used to take them out to eat on occasions. One time I wish he hadn't ...

We used to meet in town sometimes and go for lunch. My eldest daughter, who was about four years old at this point, and I were having lunch with him and he put his teeth into his hanky as per usual.

Placing them in his jacket pocket as he liked to do, we ate our steak pie and I ordered a coffee for us both. At this point the waitress is on her way over with the tray and he forgets his teeth are wrapped in his hanky and abruptly pulls it out his pocket to wipe his mouth. The dentures go flying across the table and land on the floor, much to the waitress's horror and my amusement. To make matters worse, as the waitress had now spilled our coffee on the tray with shock, he then picks them up, wipes them on the hanky and plops them in his mouth.

My daughter was screaming with laughter and I was halfway under the table. 'Grandad, your teeth are on the floor,' she kept shouting and laughing. She couldn't understand how this was possible. 'A wee wipe and they are fine,' he laughed. My daughter took ages to understand that her teeth never came out in one big block. Once I caught her in the mirror trying to lift her teeth out like he did. We spoke about this for years after and I am still laughing as I type.

On another occasion he was showing my daughter how to swing between two armchairs. You know, the stuff you tell them not to do in case they get hurt – and there's the other big kid in the room causing mischief and showing her. He fell on his arse. We still laugh about that too to this day. He left us with so many funny memories of his mischief and the times we all laughed together.

My grandad was a fit, strong working man all his days and I always thought he was a giant when I was small. It was strange to stand next to him at the same height as an adult sometimes.

I have a friend and she is very spiritual and a psychic. One day we were chatting about nonsense as usual and I said something about my grandad. 'Four,' she said. Right out the blue. I knew when messages came like this to take note. I said to her, 'Four years, that's not bad. He's on a right good run.' She replied, 'Never said years.'

Within weeks of this, my grandad had admitted he had been coughing up blood and had a bit of a cough. Her words were ringing in my ears. We went for the tests and check-ups. He was still well and up and about every day, at the bookies putting on a horse and dropping a paper off at his sister's house that was across from his every morning.

The results were back. Lung cancer, plaques on his lungs and a tumour the size of a tangerine.

As for the medical care he received I've never seen such a fucking farce in my life. After this bombshell diagnosis we were taken into a room and a young doctor passed this leaflet over for chemotherapy and said to read it and call and book what days he was going. No time to take this in, no time to make a decision. A leaflet and a fuck off.

'Hang on a minute,' I said. 'Let's get him home and take this in and then we can discuss options.' A shrug of the shoulders from the doctor then followed. I let rip. My grandad was telling me to stay calm. I know it was the shock of the news but the way that it was addressed was appalling. Yes, he was old. But chemotherapy was going to kill him. Ruin his everyday life which could be spent enjoying what he had. That should have been something that was discussed. Not just 'Here's a leaflet, that's the treatment.'

For a few months we attended for bloods, and there was no difference in his health – he was still up and about. No new symptoms. One day we went to the post office and he started having a rant about not finding me in my car. This was out of character for him. Within five minutes he was back to normal asking me to trim his hair and eyebrows and looking forward to getting in for a cup of coffee.

The following Saturday I visited with my two girls. I was going away on a course with my work and would miss his Thursday visit. He was shouting and swearing at the television, at some talent show, and my girls were laughing away at him. Again, out of character for him, but I was unaware of what was going on.

He was singing and dancing away with my youngest daughter who loved 'Ray' on this show. All the old swing songs. On the Sunday I called him for a chat before I left and I said, 'You know I love you, don't you?' He was laughing. 'You're only going away for a week. Behave yerself!!' The words were still in my head about 'four', so , from my head office while on a lunchbreak from the course I called him. No answer. Maybe he had popped out. I went through the afternoon in a haze, not taking anything in. When my course was over, I rushed to call again. No answer. I called his sister and they said he hadn't been today with the paper.

At that moment I knew . . .

Amongst the tears and snot, I was frantically calling to arrange flights home but had to get a hired car. I eventually asked his brother-in-law to call the police and the concierge of his building to force the door open. I was halfway home when I received the call.

He was gone . . . my grandad was gone.

I was not even there with him. He died alone.

It was a stroke in the brain. He had obviously been having small ones previously as I could see the changes in his behaviour. He looked like a tiny bird on the sofa. My big strong grandad, my friend . . . gone . . .

I put my coat over him, as he was in his pants and vest. He did this sometimes because it was so warm in his house.

Hours later, when the funeral home had taken him out the house, I was sitting in his chair. It was around 5 am In the morning, and I received a call from my friend, the psychic.

'He's gone,' I said

'I know, he's right here. He's showing me an apple, you have to sing the song.' The tears were pouring down my face now, but I was laughing. He was just in another place. He told her to thank me for putting my coat over him and that there was a bookie line on the table that was a winner and to give it to his brother-in-law. He also told her to get my butt off the chair and stop crying because there was a porridge pot and plate sitting in the sink needing washed.

He told her my mum came to get him. He said he was waiting until I was away. He was ready to go but not with anyone there. From the shock of the loss of him to hearing this . . . I cannot tell you the comfort I felt. I checked, and the bookie line was there, and the pot and plate were in the sink, remnants of his porridge from that morning.

My grandad hadn't left me; he was going to be around me all the time now.

Let's just say some businesses don't do customer service that well and I had a lovely funeral director step in and look after him when the first one failed, and I had a rant about that as well. A big old sweary fucking grief-stricken rant across a counter.

My daughter picked his flowers and coffin, and we arranged for a humanist to do his service in the crematorium. We played songs that reminded us of who he was. It was the loveliest way to send him off. The man he was. My Johnny . . . My grandad.

Clearing his house was heart-breaking for me. I could smell him everywhere, but as usual I got on with the task and showed no emotions.

My daughters took his chair, the chair they had sat on with him, on his knee, for as long as they had known him, a handkerchief, because there was always one in his pocket, his bunnet and his mug that he had his tea in. He wouldn't drink from any old cup, you know; it was a Rennie Mackintosh print on a bone china mug. Keepsakes, still smelling of him and his house, was what we all needed to hold on to. A little part of him.

I held it together as best as I could for my girls, but eventually it hit me. Hit me hard. He was part of the last real connection I had to my mum. I really was on my own now.

My children still do not realise to this day the tenacity they gave me to get up every day and carry on, because this could have been the part where I broke into pieces and never returned to normal (whatever the fuck normal is). A picture hangs proudly in my living room for you, Johnny. Your chair still gets used for hugs, your bunnet pressed to our faces to see if we can still smell you, and your cup held with love . . . and tea.

'Autumn Leaves' – Paolo Nutini:
https://youtu.be/fz-LU36dCr8

CHAPTER 18

All Change

I'm sure I had delayed grief, but I had been exhausted, juggling work and the care of the kids. I felt overwhelmed in a job that was full of liars and bullshitters. I missed my grandad badly. I felt more alone than I had ever in my life ...

I wanted change, so, as usual, I changed something. My job.

My new job entailed having a live-in apartment, and I had sat down and discussed it with my daughters. My eldest was moving into a flat with her friend, and my youngest decided she would live with her dad and I would do weekends etc. 'It's just like swapping, Mum.'

It was that easy for her. It wasn't for me.

As much as I tried to enjoy the space and the change to work on finding myself, I missed them both so much it hurt my heart. I found myself changing: I stopped wearing suits, stopped straightening my hair and let it dry in its natural curly state. I was connecting with my spiritual side – reiki, meditation and walks in nature.

I was in one of the loveliest parts of Scotland and I was still fucking lost.

The grass was not any greener. So, I changed it ... again. This repeated behaviour of detachment and avoidance has continued for a long time. I just thought I was brave, maybe I was just taking action when things did not feel right? People will have their opinions on this, but I just knew what was right to do for myself.

I came back to Glasgow and signed up for the rat race once again. It seemed the bigger plan was not to be. I then injured my neck, and it floored me for months. Other health problems had arisen for me too, and I struggled for the next year, quite ill, with no answers.

Moving again, now out of Scotland, I went back to work and led an enjoyable life in Wales. It was a peaceful and safe place for my daughter, but my health was still challenging for me and I wanted to be near my eldest daughter and my friends.

It was time to come home to Glasgow. There was shit that needed sorted. Shit that I never knew about myself that was now coming to the fore.

'Coming Home' – Sigma and Rita Ora:
https://youtu.be/tS26xch5U24

Part Three

CHAPTER 19

The Police

October 2012. I was back in Glasgow and I was sitting on my bed trying to dry my hair. I could hardly lift the hairdryer because of the pain and swelling in my joints and in my arms.

A large towel was wrapped around me and I felt vulnerable, inept and unable to cope with everyday tasks. My health was horrific.

The list was long: angioedema, urticaria, painful joints, colitis, neuropathic pain. My liver was struggling to get rid of the excess toxins in my body and I had no answers after going around all the relevant departments in the hospital. I was a puzzle to them. I showed autoimmune symptoms but none matched the textbook tests for lupus or rheumatoid arthritis.

My thoughts were dark. 'What If I get worse? What if I die? My concerns were my two daughters. 'How could they cope if they lost their mamma?'

Suddenly, the thought of PFB came into my head. I wondered if he was getting on with his life with no issues while and here I was, still suffering from the damage he had caused. It did not feel fair that he had continued in his career and had remarried.

Here I was, wondering if all my symptoms were psychosomatic because of what he had done. Was it all in my head? Was it somatisation, the effects of the emotional poison I was carrying affecting my physical health? Was my body processing the toxic thoughts he left me with? Was I swelling because I couldn't bear to be touched? Did my skin crawl and break out in hives because of where he touched me?

Getting up off the bed, I made my way to the phone and took

a breath. I looked up the local police station and called. I asked if there was a female unit available to report sexual assault. The guy had no clue; there was nothing of that sort in the local police station but he went and got information for another station who handled this type of thing. Calling the other number, I was shaking.

Its time ...

Time someone else heard what PFB had done and dealt with it through the legal system.

A male officer answered the phone.

'Family protection unit?'

'I want to report someone for sexual assault when I was a child,' I said it. The process had started.

Brusque and unsympathetic, he asked for my details, details of the accused and started to ask some questions about the abuse.

What the fuck is wrong with this picture? I thought.

Where was the calm tone and the gentle manner, the offer of a referral over to a woman if I needed it? I stopped him in his tracks.

'I'd rather I could speak to a woman and make an appointment to come in. This is not something I wanted to discuss on the phone,' I said.

Frontline staff answering phones without one ounce of compassion or reassurance. Boy did the expectation of this being easy get shattered in that moment.

It is the bravest call many women and men need to make on their own behalf or for a daughter/son, friend, sister or brother, and yet it was official and brusque.

My appointment was booked to go over to the station the following Saturday. It was in a part of Glasgow near PFB's house, apparently, as I found out later.

You really couldn't make this shit up!

I later called my sister to tell her I had called the police, and I was in tears. It was like a release of a coiled spring in my body, making that call to the police, like the weight of dragging this around all this time was finally detaching itself from me. She was a bit shocked as this was out the blue. This issue had not been spoken about since my early twenties when I brought it up before, then was forgotten about. I was now forty years old.

I knew it would be hard for her to hear my pain but, I lived with this every day. It was the present for me. There was nothing historical about the pain, the triggers, memories that crept into your daily life when you see someone that has the same nose or hands. When you smell certain things and that part of your brain where smell memory association jumps into life, taking you back to that specific memory. I had to leave a trolley of shopping in a supermarket one day and walk outside because someone walked by with the stink of TCP on them.

Boom . . . it would come out of nowhere. It did not care what social situation you were in. It burst to the forefront of your consciousness and attacked your senses. Grabbing this fucker and dragging it back to the box it was hidden in was like fighting with a tiger under the table as you were eating a steak he wanted.

Not showing what's going on under the surface is the hardest task you face daily, so that no one sees your pain, your confusion, the feelings of disgust. It is hard to tell anyone about this and, as I have experienced, sometimes people can and will and use it against you, for their own benefit of revenge, to call you unhinged and justify their own behaviour, when you shared it with them or told them in confidence. That will not be forgotten or forgiven . . .

20/10/2012 and 21/10/2012
I had two days of interviews over ten hours with an appointed SOLO, or Sexual Offences Liaison Officer. It included questions, descriptions. It involved opening the files of hidden pain and pulling up the memories and trying to explain to the police the

surrounding circumstances and the bullying, control and manipulation within the surrounding family situation. I had to make them understand that PFB's family helped facilitate what he had done, especially FM.

Unfortunately I soon learned that, at least for that officer, feelings and other things did not matter. What PFB had done, the times, my age, the places, was what was needed. I also gave them a copy of my dated book I had tried to write many years before, hoping that this corroborated my story on this being an ongoing issue and not an accusation out of the blue.

It was exhausting, and I was glad when it was over. I remembered what I could at the time, and more memories have resurfaced since. The can of worms was opened.

The police now had my statement and the officer who took the statement stayed on as my SOLO to continue the trust. Witnesses took time to be interviewed. That was how the 'process' went.

My father gave a statement of that time that I had disclosed to him in my twenties. FM, FS and BFB were interviewed (FF had passed away by then).

My younger brother refused to give a statement. Well, why would he want to give one? He was still part of their 'family', yet he admitted years earlier that he always remembered ringing the doorbell and no one answering straight away, while PFB's motorbike was outside, he knew. Whatever reason he has for not giving a statement, that is for him to deal with. Not my issue, everyone has choices, free will.

It was the following August, in 2013, before PFB was brought in and questioned and charged. Considering I'd started the process in October 2012, if you go thinking this will be over quickly, it won't. It is a long, drawn-out process.

He used the law to make sure there was no corroboration used from anything he may have said in the interview. He said 'No comment' like he was advised to by his solicitor (Cadder ruling).

He was charged with three charges of lewd and libidinous practice. The charges met the time period of when the crimes had happened.

Three charges.

He was released on a bail undertaking, with the conditions that he would not contact me, and nor would his family.

I was then told that there would be a petition at court on 4th October 2013.

From what I was led to believe, this is the part where the evidence is presented to the PF (procurator fiscal) from the police and he pleads guilty or not guilty. Further evidence can then be sourced and gathered for trial.

The procurator fiscal (or PF for short, Scotland's version of a public prosecutor) now had the charge sheet and my statement but asked the police to gather further evidence and interview witnesses.

The police contacted me to tell me they would be interviewing witnesses but the evidence the PF had requested was not notified to me until January 2014, and I said for them to come over and get it as I had recently received social work notes giving as much proof as they needed of this, so these would save them wasting time looking for it. I also provided a photo of myself when I was small and a photo of me and other family members including PFB.

Five months earlier, PFB he had been charged and this was me now finding out from the police – there had been no hearing yet at court on that date, or any further one arranged. The PF needed even more information, I was told. I wrote to them asking when this would happen. I got no reply.

I felt gutted. Why was he not at court? Why had no one updated me since this had been delayed? Five months. I assumed the hearing had taken place and he had pleaded not guilty and that more evidence was being collected for trial. No one had told me otherwise and I had no one guiding me through this process and its legal steps.

The information sat on a desk in the police station for another twelve weeks. It went nowhere.

I called the PF in Glasgow and asked why they had requested this but did not have it.

Their answer was 'Police have not sent it.'

I called the police; they said, 'The PF has not requested it yet.'

The right hand not knowing what the left is doing.

I took the bull by the horns and gathered the information I had given to the police, and along with this I wrote a victim statement to the PF and sent it recorded delivery, so they had no excuse to say it was lost in the post.

The statement was to let them know I was not scared to stand in court and that I would be willing to truthfully back up everything that I had said to the police. I wouldn't be behind a screen, I told them, and I would face PFB. I also requested that they get access to the full social work files to see the bigger picture of this toxic situation in the foster home as I had only received limited information about myself in my notes. I asked for a date when the petition would be happening.

No reply.

The police apparently got that request and picked the full case notes up from social work and handed them in to the PF.

At this point my SOLO went off sick and there were times she was on a course. I could barely get her when I needed updates. It had already been a challenge to get hold of her sometimes as she had her day job to do and courses to go on. I've no issue with that. Her job is vitally important to others, especially children.

Another team member took over and called to introduce himself and to ask for further proof the PF needed. I was surprised and disappointed at his request – I had provided it already.

He said he would check the file and get back to me. He never did. I again had to make the calls to him to get updates, but none came. Something was not sitting right with me, but hey, if you've made it this far with this book, you'll know that the real information always comes out later. I asked if the social work file had been also handed to the PF. He didn't know.

I called the PF again to make sure they had the full social work file that the police had picked up from the council before my original SOLO went off sick.

I was told, 'It's there for Crown Counsel to use should they decide to do so.'

WTF?

This file was important in showing the surrounding toxic family situation I lived in, which I was not allowed to see as parts had been redacted.

'If they choose'. I was still reeling at this. I assumed this was important evidence and could be used.

The crime-reporting setup for victims in Scotland was a disgrace at the time when I came forward. England has set teams and processes. I did most of the work and made the calls. That was not my job.

Any further requests of information from the police were met by 'Call the PF for an update'. Once the police have done the first investigation and supplied further evidence for the PF, it's no longer their remit.

One thing I did find out later was that the police could have made a referral to the NMC regarding the charges against PFB because he was a registered nurse. They never did.

Somebody with information and full names of police officers involved (which I had no idea of) – went to the newspapers. The *Sunday Mail* was to run a story on a man being charged, and the police SOLO informed me of this as their press office was dealing with it. I stayed up all night and drove to a local garage to get the first edition and later another edition. There was no story. I will never know if this was due to a legal issue or someone stopping the story going to print through their solicitor.

My anonymity was not breached.

Within my statement to the police I had described an incident in England and in Spain. I was told the details would also be passed to Yorkshire police and Interpol as this was their jurisdiction. I was never contacted by either.

My experience was appalling, But I have opened my mouth now, and that felt good.

'Warrior' – Demi Lovato: https://youtu.be/UFeJkfB4xKo

CHAPTER 20

Social Work Notes

I never knew there were files and notes when a child was in care, and when I found this out I thought it would be a good idea to try and get them, maybe find some answers about the reasons for being taken into care etc. I should have had a copy of them when I left my care placement, but it was never given.

In 2007 I contacted a member of staff from the fostering section of the council. I requested my social work notes and had a meeting with this person to look over them.

A few bits and pieces from when I left the care of the children's home were available, showing some grants and housing applied for. I was told the rest of my file was missing, that someone had signed it out. I made the social worker aware that the foster placement had been horrendous, and I needed information. There was nothing he could do, he said.

I left it at that. I had read stories of other people trying to get their notes and it had been the same scenario. I was putting it down to time passing.

Five years later, in 2012, after I had been to the police to report PFB, I requested – via an email to the guy I spoke to previously – that the social work department had a further look for these notes. The email was never answered.

I had to then contact a different department, and in February 2013 I received a file with some more notes in it, detailing older documents but some parts were blacked out as these did not pertain to me.

Within the covering letter, the department stated that a previous statement from them of a file being missing was a mix-up with the way the records had been managed and archived.

It was a family file, all together as I had two siblings in the same foster placement. Yet I had left this foster family, so a separate file would have been opened from when I was in the care of the children's home. That's what the previous guy from the fostering team had stated.

He said it had been 'signed out'.

My paranoia was off the scale at this point as I knew I had no reason for my file to be signed out at any point as I had no police or social work involvement ever.

Further investigation led me to find out that PFB had worked with lots of social work offices around Glasgow due to his job. Had he gotten access to them because he was worried that there may be something in there that came back and bit him and his family on the backside years later? I will never know.

What I found in that file shocked me to the core.

This was probably one of the toughest times in my adult life, reading the social work department notes about me as a child.

The fact that everything that happened to me could have been avoided if the social work department had done their job properly, made me sick.

I believed that I still had a father with legal rights and that I was fostered out to my dad's family, who had welcomed me gladly, straight after my mother had passed. I thought the fostering was the result of an amicable agreement between my father and aunt. Visits from a social worker in my childhood had been few and far between, and the kids at school who had social workers were usually truanting from school or had gotten into trouble etc. I was previously unaware of the truth, the law, the social work acts and their obligations, but that was now going to get very clear.

Here it goes ...

1. Placed into care from the Pollok social work office after mother's death on 29.6.1974 under a voluntary Section 15.

This meant that at any time a family member or friend could have taken us back out of that children's home at any time. Only stipulation on the Section 15 was that we had to be brought up in the same religious manner as our parents would have wanted – nothing else, just that.

2. Three months later after no one, including my father or maternal grandparents removed us from this home, which we were still in voluntarily, a committee meeting was undertaken one afternoon on 24.9.1974.

No children's panel, just a meeting. I bet the fuckers had tea and cakes ...

3. I was then, along with my siblings, placed under Section 16 of the Social Work Act 1968.

The local authority by law had a duty to show the performance of their functions within this act. Here's a small section of it:

Social Work Act 1968
Part 4 (a) 1 recording by the local Authority of information relating to those whom persons are boarded out.
(b) For securing person who is and the place where he is boarded out by the local authority is supervised and inspected by the local authority and that he shall be removed from this place in question if his welfare requires it.

This bit should have been adhered to when the school called the social work department about my assault.

I had also found out that my dad had contacted the social work department to ask for a letter stating that they took us from him and that he did not 'sign us over' into care, to prove to us that he had done nothing wrong. He had taken the blame for years and wanted to prove he was not the one that made the decision. I explained that I had been looking for social work notes and he said he used to have a letter that showed he was not responsible for putting us into care, but my brother had taken it and binned it.

A copy of the previous letter arrived in February 2013. It had originally been sent to him on 17th June 2011.

I had no contact with him at that time and I never knew of the letter's existence.

I met with him on 4th December 2012 – my mum's birthday of all days.

It stated:

I have not at this stage been able to locate documentation specifically relating to the circumstances surrounding the children being taken into care, in any case it's their information and could not provide it to you.

It then goes on to say:

Our records indicate that the local authority assumed parental rights for the children in accordance with the Section 16 of the Social Work Act 1968. Copy enclosed for your information.

WTF? Assumed parental rights? First I had ever been aware of this.

You will note that the legislation enabled the LA to assume parental rights for a child if a parent was deceased or unable or unfit to look after the child.

It was not dependant on the child being 'signed over' by a parent to the LA but rather dependant on whether circumstances warranted the LA assuming parental rights.

You will also note from the copy of the legislation that a person may object to the local authority assuming parental rights. Our records indicate that when the local authority assumed parental rights for the children you sought custody of the children through the legal process.

The social work department contested your application on the grounds that at the time you had persistently failed to exercise your responsibilities as a parent.

The Court considered the matter and ruled against your application for custody and the children remained under the supervision of the LA.

So ...

Under Section 16 (B) part v it states:

Has so persistently failed without reasonable cause to discharge the obligation of a parent or guardian to be unfit as to have the care of the child.

This was the section highlighted on the copy they sent to my dad

Parts 2 and 3 of this copy also state that, as per its legal duty, the LA

shall forthwith after the passing of the resolution serve on him, the person on whose account the resolution was passed serves on him a notice in writing on the LA objecting to the resolution.

So, these fuckers can decide and then send a letter to say they have done it and if you want to object do so within fourteen days?

It also states on Section 5 of this that

> *Any notice under this section may be served by post, so however that a notice served by a LA under subsection (2) of this section shall not be duly served unless it is sent in a registered letter or by recorded delivery service.*

The letter came after they made the decision. No copy of this letter in my files or any proof that it was sent registered either? No proof at the legal department archives of the council either.

Part 3 states:

> *the LA may not later than 14 days from the receipt of them of the notice, apply by way of summary application against the objection to the resolution to the sheriff having jurisdiction in the area of the LA and in that event the resolution shall not lapse by reason of the service until the determination of the application and the sheriff may on the hearing of the application order that the resolution shall not lapse by reason of the service of the notice.*

The LA had 14 days to get that in front of a sheriff and reject my dad's objection.

Now at this point it's three months after my mother's death, Dad was a mess, still drinking.

Fair?

My father said he did get legal advice but was told it was too late and so he did nothing further. The letter stated he objected and applied for custody, but I checked the National Archives for proof of what he said and what the letter said, and I requested a file – Sc36/55/14-21 of the social work records of Glasgow Sheriff Court to be exact, which covered the social work applications for 1974 and early 1975.

There was no mention of me in it.

No trace of application by my father or Glasgow City Council. No trace of me, or my siblings' names there either.

This was also confirmed by email from a member of the National Archives staff, just to make sure I had not missed anything when I had investigated myself.

My next step was to then ask Glasgow City Council to provide a copy of this registered letter they would legally have had to send to my father, and a copy of their application to the sheriff. Fair?

The reply I got was:

> *No separate legal file has been located. But I have sight of the social work file which relates to the committee meeting at which it was resolved in terms of Section 16 of the social work act and that the local authority assumed parental rights over you and your siblings. Social work and health committee dated 24th September 1974 which corresponds to the assumption of rights and enclose a copy for your information.*
>
> *I have discussed the case with my colleagues in GCC* [Glasgow City Council's] *legal department and it is deemed unlikely that a separate legal file would have been created unless the assumption of parental rights had been contested in court.*

So, the letter to my dad stated one thing, yet the records, archives and legal file were not available to prove this.

So, my life in care started with a fucking one-page document. I was owned by an authority, no longer part of a family.

The council were now legally my parents, by law. Not

common law – statutory law, by their own choice to take that role on.

The top part of the copy they provided me shows the assumption of parental rights for 9 children. numbers SW 202, SW 203 and SW 204.

That was it, a number.

That was how easy it was to take three children from a parent when another one dies.

I also asked for any notes pertaining to the other two children's homes that I had been in to see if there was any further information within them that could help give me information.

I received the following reply:

I have searched both the Records Management and Archive holdings for records relating to your time placed in [name omitted] and later in [name omitted]. There are no records for either home in the archive holdings. There are some in the Record Management holdings, but these are not relevant to the time you were placed there. They relate to the finance, maintenance or conveyancing of the building rather than to the care of the individual placed there.

So, I had no notes from my two children's home placements either?

But let's go back over this.

I was placed in this children's home, three months voluntary on a Section 15 from **31.6.1974** until **24.9.1974**, and then another twelve months under the Section 16 that had been passed.

Three small children left in a home for fifteen months – and where was the family?

Fostered on **21.9.75**.

The boarding out regulations covered this in cases of

children being fostered out: regular visits, reports, updates, checks done.

Not a chance.

First visit: three years and six months since being fostered!

The notes I received stated:

> *This office failed to give any support to the foster home in the first few years until the case was picked up by Joan Watson, social worker at _____, who visited **21.3.1979** and was met with quite a bit of aggression on Mrs FM's part.*

Verbatim on the notes.

The next visit date was not shown on the notes but stated at the end they would revisit in **April 1982, in 6 months' time.**

Second visit:

November 1981. 2 years and 8 months after the first visit.

Second visit notes are all about FM's own children doing so well ... blah blah, family time together, but she did find it a strain taking the responsibility for everything as her husband was a foreman and worked late hours ...

9-5. He was a foreman and he was home most nights for 6 pm, no weekend work. It was all lies. I served his dinner and washed the dishes, so I know he was there every night. It went on:

> *Children recently renewed contact with maternal grandparents and got some answers regarding sisters questioning about her mother.*
>
> *'Mrs FM could not furnish [sibling 1] with any facts about her mother, grandparents filling the gaps.*

Yes because, as I said earlier, my mother did not have much contact or time for my father's family or have anything to do with them. FM's family were strangers to us, and she was my aunt by DNA only, through my father.

FM conveniently forgot to mention that my sister ran away and landed on my grandparents' doorstep and the reason contact was re-established with them – which was that she had demanded to get visits started for all of us.

Third visit: 20.04.1983. One year and five months after the second visit.

The record showed that we now had a new social worker, as well as some general notes as usual about how well we were doing.

Not one set of notes from these visits was directed or undertaken on our behalf. They were all controlled by FM and her version of events.

The next visit was when I got the belt and the school called the social work department and asked for my social worker as I had no clue who it was. This was around **1986**, my second year in high school.

Bear in mind that this was not a visit arranged by social work; this was the school contacting them. This was the first time I had ever seen the new social worker, the messy-haired tramp guy I'd mentioned before. The next time I saw him was when I ran away from the foster home and never returned, at fifteen years old.

So, where was he after the running away incident and then the belt assault?

Did he come out and check on me? No, not a return visit or check-up to make sure I was safe. Lazy wee prick!

Their recording procedures, record-keeping, removal from the placement if it requires doing so in the interests of the child, by law were all ignored.

It was all there in the notes, provided by them, to me. It was a total fuck-up from start till finish under their parental rights the council had assumed. All of this can be confirmed and verified by copies of emails and letters. The social work notes are all there too.

I now also had another set of notes also provided by the records I had requested. This covered the time after I was put into the children's home at fifteen years old.

What follows is the written notes from my social worker I had after I was placed into the children's home. I'm guessing the messy-haired tramp had left or was just reassigned another case to swerve.

10.5.88

Introductory visit to meet Mr FF and Mrs FM and introduce myself as the new social worker.

Mr FF and Mrs FM made it clear that they blamed social work dept for Katy's removal into _____ children's home.

They felt that the SWD had allowed Katy to abuse the system by demanding that she be removed out of the Foster Family household.

So, they were good at throwing about the word 'abuse' to accuse a child, but they won't utter it when it's about their son?

Essentially the problems were related to Katy feeling that the [foster parents] were too strict e.g. school uniform and had to be in the house at certain times.

This was the FM's and FF's reasons for me leaving, not my statement.

Katy found it difficult to get on with their son and she felt that [her siblings] and herself were treated differently from the rest of the family.

This was probably the only time I ever mentioned this, hoping they would ask further details. They didn't.

At a subsequent childcare review Katy refused to go back home with the Foster family and the decision was that she be admitted to the children's home.'

An attempt was made at the meeting thereafter for [the foster family] and Katy to reconcile their differences, but this ended with Mr (FF) walking out of the review.

Overall Mr and Mrs (FF) and (FM's) feelings are that up until this incident involving Katy, they had received little support from the SWD and when the SWD did become involved the situation was made worse.

In discussions with [sibling 2], he felt that now [sibling 1] and Katy were now out of the house, he felt in a difficult position and has divided loyalties and is beginning according to Mrs (FM) to vocalise threats to her that he will come down to the SWD and ask to get taken into a children's home as Katy did.

At present, the involvement from SWD was minimal – they preferred to get on without too much contact with the dept but knew that if there were any problems to contact us.

Assessment

The overall impression from this couple was that they wanted as little to do with the SWD as possible.

However, their complaints about SWD involvement had a lot of truth.

They seem not to be willing to take any responsibility for the situation with Katy. They were not prepared to accept that at least in the past perhaps they needed to compromise more

Essentially [sibling 1], Katy and [sibling 2] had to meet their standards or else – however I do suspect they were

also equally as strict with their own family although they might have been able to accept it more.

They impress as a couple who need to be very much in control and rather rigid in their attitudes.

Obviously fostering long term even if it is related is an artificial situation and there will be difficulties.

Problem is that often foster parents feel that if they admit there are problems this is then seen as a failure.

However, it is now interesting to note that [sibling 1], Katy and now [sibling 2] are making clear statements that the [foster family's] regime is too strict, or perhaps they have outgrown the family situation as it is often the case in ordinary family situations.

Plans

1.   To maintain minimal contact with Mr FF and Mrs FM – offer support when needed.
2.   Maintain contact with [sibling 2] as needed.
3.   [Blacked out by Records Dept. I'm not allowed to see this part.]

There you go. Minimal contact at their own admission, controlling who knew what went on in their home. Social worker admitting that the previous contact had been minimal overall impression they wanted as little to do with SWD as possible? Absolutely, it was all about their control.

So why not tell them that by law you had a duty to visit and record anything in the interests of the children that you assumed parental rights for? That the decision was not theirs to make, it was yours?

'Very much in control, rigid, meet their standards or else'? Did you not ask what 'or else' meant?

The saddest part was at the end, assuming we may have just outgrown the family situation as in ordinary family situations

... Really? Maybe it was because if one of you had turned up for a fucking change and we might have had an earlier chance to speak.

How many kids do you know in an ordinary family situation that constantly ran away – one left, then another was placed into a home, and now the remaining child was threatening to leave too? Even though the above assessment was about the best I had seen on paper so far in my notes, the situation was still not investigated further. No more questions were asked. No interviews. The first step on the plan was not even about the existing child in their care, it was about keeping in contact with the FF and FM ...

These notes confirmed to me that what I felt about the social work was true: The department was complicit in letting FM do what she wanted, her rules, her way, same as she was complicit in ignoring her son's behaviour.

This is not over ...

'Listen' – Beyoncé: https://youtu.be/RmGe-LY5HQs

CHAPTER 21

Psycho the Rapist

That is what I read when I see the letter has arrived for my first appointment. Psycho-the-rapist.

My doctor had referred me to a psychotherapist because we had no answers about my health and we decided together that maybe the symptoms could be psychosomatic from disclosing the abuse and being back in Glasgow again. My symptoms had progressively worsened since I had come back to live here.

The issue we had though was that even though I had reported PFB to the police, I was not aware if he was still working within the psychiatric field in and around Glasgow so I could not get a referral to the usual local place.

The place I was referred to was five minutes from my childhood foster home, from the frying pan into the fire.

First the police station being next to PFB's home, and now this.

I felt like telling them to shove their appointment, but my anxiety had been bad recently and I had started cleaning obsessively, looking for dirt that was not there. Picking up bits of fluff from the carpet and deciding to vacuum over and over. I needed help, needed tools to control my behaviour as the anti-depressant route was not an option. I was not depressed. I was reacting to my situation. Beta blockers helped slightly with the palpitations and took some of the edge off the anxiety, but I needed this sorted.

This was horrific. My mind was going mental with the thoughts of keeping the place clean and in order, and physically I could hardly lift my arms. My feet were throbbing when I walked and my muscles ached.

My face was swollen and distorted. I struggled to wear clothes as any pressure on my skin hurt and started the angioedema (swelling).

But anything to keep my mind off the other thoughts that were coming forward tenfold – the smells, the feelings of pain.

Between sleeping I would sometimes crawl around the floors, wiping with a cloth, tears running down my face at my exhaustion and pain in my body but battling this to overcome the excessive, almost manic need to clean.

Maybe I was thinking, on some level, that if my surroundings were clean and organised then so would I be.

My home became my prison as I struggled to go out and leave the safe space that was my home. When I did – on rare occasions and only when important – I would play the part and get dressed. Wash and dry my hair. Look like a normal person for a day. It might only have been an hour appointment with the solicitor or doctor, but it rendered me exhausted the rest of the day.

Most days I would be in pyjamas. Hair scraped back after washing, isolated and alone. Angry that no one in the medical field knew what was up with me.

I went to the appointment, passing by the main road, past the old house where my foster placement was, and sat in the waiting room with others. 'I shouldn't be here,' I said to myself. 'There are others with real issues sitting here and I'm taking their appointment time.' True, I wasn't rocking in a chair and had crazy hair – but it's not always about what you can see or what others see. Sometimes the pain is buried so well you can look as normal as anyone else – if there is even such a thing as normal.

The psychotherapist came out to call me in. I entered the room, explained in brief my past and the recent notes landing on my door. The hour was over. Boom.

Fuck.

Another appointment was given.

I left feeling a little gutted that it would maybe take time to process the background of my issues before I then got the right therapy to deal with it.

I missed the next appointment due to my health being bad.

Another appointment came along, and more of the story was told. But this time I did ask for some tools to cope. CBT – cognitive behavioural therapy – was the answer, apparently. It was explained to me how it helps and that this would come later. Fuck that, I thought. I went home and ordered a book on it and started to read it ASAP, looking for the fix ...

The following appointment was cancelled as the therapist was off. No one called. I was pissed right off. Standing at the reception being told that my appointment was not happening was triggering my anxiety badly. Each time I had to go there it set off higher feelings of anxiety, sending me back to that area where it all had happened.

Previous times when I wanted to ask for help when I felt so low, the thought of my kids being affected stopped me doing this. I was their mum. I had to be strong and if I showed any weakness it made me a failure. That was what was in my head – and the fear of social work becoming involved and my kids at risk of fuck-ups from a department that caused my pain. Over my dead body was social work going to ever interfere in my children's lives.

They were now fourteen and twenty-two and had their own voices. Friends around me, a supportive ex-partner and my youngest's school could all back up the fact that my kids were not at risk. Accepting that this time I could not just get up and put my smiley face on, it was a relief to be heard at last and not judged.

Another appointment day had arrived and I had gotten the day wrong. Something was not right; it was like the universe was telling me not to be there. My gut feeling was that this was not the place to be going. But there was no other place to go. This therapy was also limited to every three weeks for an hour. I needed more than that.

So, I did what I usually do. I said, 'Shove it.'

Realising yet again that it was hard to trust others to help, I went back to that protective place where I buried my pain and feelings and put the smiley face on.

I later found out the mother of one of PFB's children worked at that therapy office. My gut was not wrong.

I saw a private psychiatrist, no medication needed, and was told cognitive behavioural therapy would help, and that was my prescription. I sent a copy of this assessment to the police and procurator fiscal too. It was yet more evidence to refute the mental health and bipolar allegations from FM and PFB and their supporters. I was damaged but not fucking crazy. Time to heal, my own way, free myself from what was holding me back for so many years.

'Breathing Underwater' – Emeli Sandé:
https://youtu.be/ye-3d2QCz2o

CHAPTER 22

Father

I had not seen my dad for ten years. The last contact had been when my youngest was about four years old, and that was brief.

I needed to go and see him and get some answers. I had released my truth to the police and was on a journey to healing everything that had eaten me alive emotionally. Now was the time to get some information.

4th December 2012. I arrived at his door, he opened it and he said, 'Can I help you?'

'It's Kathleen, your daughter …'

He never even knew who I was. 'Come in,' he said, and I entered his house. He looked old and tiny.

When he realised it was me in the light of the living room, he was visibly upset.

I came straight to the point and told him I was there to get information about my mum and my past, that I had ongoing health problems and I was sure they were hereditary, and I needed to know what he was suffering from.

We discussed many things in my visits during the weeks that followed. He would joke and wander off into other stories.

I watched him sitting on his machine, gasping for breath, taking his medication. I wanted to be careful and not get too involved emotionally, but I needed the answers. It *was* emotional. I was finding out some more of the real story while I was there chatting. He was old, he was unwell, he was still my dad. I was so torn between trying to distance myself from him as my dad, and compassion for the human being he was. It was a time I will never forget; emotions were torn apart and confusing but I was happy in knowing I got to know him a little better.

A photo album was put together for him for Christmas, along with a picture of my mum that he wanted copied from my house. He kept it in the drawer, which I found strange. I had left half of the album empty so he could fill it with pictures of his other daughters and grandchild, who was soon to be born.

The photo was hidden in the drawer because he did not want his daughters seeing it. The album was stored in a wardrobe. I could understand that he did not want them upset or feeling pushed out. All I wanted to do was give him some memories. To show we were all doing well regardless of the circumstances. We were all his family. There was no 'them' and 'us' for me.

I offered advice on some things I had been using to help with ongoing health issues of my own and I left him some magnesium oil to spray on his skin.

The medication he was taking was making no difference some days. He decided to drop the amount of co-codamol he was taking every day because his mind was getting clearer and he wanted no more drugs to cloud his head. I visited his doctor with him and told him of the alternative things we had been trying. His doctor said he had never seen him so fit and well. Little did I know these offers of help given would come back and bite me on the arse.

It was tough going: his personality would change if I questioned parts of his story that changed on numerous occasions. He would say, 'It's the brain damage with the drink.'

I was exhausted emotionally and physically and had grave concerns for his mental health some days, and then other days he would be as normal as you expect for a man of his age.

His daughter from his second marriage was in one day when I visited. We had some chats about lots of things. She said that her own grandad had tried to get her mum and our dad a house so that they could take us into their care, but her mum was eighteen at the time and my brother was ten, so she was just eight years older. This was all new to me. I gave her a hug when she left and there seemed to be no issue between us, but I never expected to hear what I did later.

Christmas was tough. My dad had hinted he had nowhere to go, but I knew he was lying. His ex-wife had invited him, and he had forgotten he had told me this previously. Later in the day my youngest and I popped in to see him with some food. I had decided to have a quiet day. No big family dinners today, we wanted to do Christmas our way, so we had a breakfast all together, then pyjamas and films with a tin of Quality Street.

He said that the cards and gifts I left for his daughters were unopened. 'They wanted fuck all from you,' he said. I was pretty taken aback at this. I asked him what the aggression was all about.

'I gave them less this year for Christmas and they are raging,' he said. So that was it, I had received £150 in a card for my two girls and I, so £50 each. I would have given the money back for them if it mattered that much, but again, I was not sure if this was my dad playing games or if it was true. There's no point in causing a drama over money, so I said nothing. I wanted no fight with any of them, if what my dad said was even true in the first place. I understand their reluctance to accept a gift from someone that had never been there as a sister.

In January 2013, my father and I attended a cousin's funeral together. I was there to say goodbye to a beautiful young woman taken too early. I knew many members of the family would be there. I nearly didn't go, but I was going to show respect and say goodbye – no one was stopping me doing that. I am sure my presence shocked a few people. A certain someone stood with his head down and turned away every time I caught his eye. This was not the time or the place. He would know why I was around in a little while. I am sure questions were asked as to why I was suddenly there with my father. Someone then gave a ridiculous reason.

My younger brother (allegedly) decided to tell everyone he had started a rumour that my father had won £1.2 million on the lottery and that's why I was now hanging about him. Unbeknown to him, I had been around since December 2012.

My father told me of this, and I laughed. How far from the truth was that? My concern was that if he was spreading this rumour to hurt me, then the only person that was at risk of being hurt was my dad, a housebound invalid, unable to fight anyone off that came to rob him. If he'd spread that rumour, that was a pretty low blow. I never knew what truth was and what was real when my dad spoke; he was good at playing games to get what he needed – love, company, adoration. He had done this all his life.

The conversations with my dad continued to run away into other stories. He had told me many personal things about other people and at this point I started getting a little wary. If he could accuse others of stealing from him and give out personal details, would he do the same with me? My gut was niggling.

He had hidden money in his house and asked me to hold onto it for him. Each time he wanted things bought, I stored the receipts with his money and made a list of what had been bought and what was left of the money. I asked him to look over it when he visited. He declined. He kept saying, 'Just use it if you need it.' I took nothing from it. It felt like he was trying to make up for never being there by offering me money now, but my reluctance to take anything from him stemmed from the accusations he had made about others. I wanted nothing but the truth, not his money, but it seemed his version of events was so clouded by the damage the drink had done to his brain, I knew I was getting nowhere fast.

The trips up and down when I could go were tough. I organised an occupational therapist and had some adjustments made for him at home: a walk-in shower, buzzers for door entry at his chair, and a mechanical bed raiser. He had a clean house and healthy food. He still wanted more from me. I was tired, and my own health was bad. I stopped going so much, and that's when it all changed. Up until then, he would text me every day –

'Good morning' – that stopped. Instead he'd make remarks like 'Don't worry about me, I am ill in bed.' He'd switch his mobile phone off and refuse to answer his house phone. I was stunned and shocked at the change in his manner, confused at his actions.

It was February 2013, and I visited him armed with my notes from social work so we could go over them. My dad had written to request another copy of the letter from social work. He also stated that he had kicked in the door of the home we were in and tried to take us out of there and he had been removed by the police. *No record of this.*

He told me that my grandad had put us all in care – dumped us at the social work department, then he accused my grandad of going that night to my gran's cousin's house and getting pissed: 'Yer granny put a bottle of whisky over his head that night, he had a cut on his head the day of your mammy's funeral.'

His youngest daughter was there during this conversation. She confirmed she had been told this too.

Not fucking true though, was it?

The bottom dropped out of my world ... My wonderful grandad had put us in care?

My friend, my confidante for years – my only source of constant family from when I was fifteen years old till the day he died – had put me in the hands of social workers?

I never expected this venom from him I had to leave. I wasn't there to accuse or blame. I just needed answers, but he was on the defensive. As I was leaving, my father shouted words I'll never forget, which cut me in half:

'Wisnae me that put you in care. Yer old granda done it.' That's when I saw a side to my father I never wanted to see. He knew how close I had been to my grandad and had no concern for my relationship with him, or his memory. He was only concerned with being vindicated. I had always thought I was in this situation because my dad put us in care. He had been blamed for years. He had every right to be hurt and defensive if I'd got it wrong, but to deliver it in such a caustic way with no regard for how I felt was wrong.

I called my sister in tears and told her of the accusation my dad had made. She admitted she knew this, and so did my older brother.

All these fucking years of not knowing the circumstances while they both knew, and said nothing. My emotions were all over the place. First finding out the things in the social work notes – and now this? I felt ignored and shut out. Was I ever going to get the full story? Being the last to know seemed like the norm now.

It all came to a head the following Saturday. My dad had an upset stomach and demanded I go to the chemist and get him something. I text back I was at the hospital A and E and would call him later. No response. Another text came. It was hurtful.

I said I would go later. I did.

I walked in and he was sitting with the blinds closed. He had paperwork strewn everywhere. He had a story to write, he said. I'd previously organised all his old bags of paperwork and photos into a set of plastic drawers for him, and now the drawers were open, and he sat in his housecoat in the dark. I knew something was wrong. I stood looking at him with tears in my eyes. He was ranting at me, saying I was a mental case and everyone knew I was poisoning him with my herbal concoctions. He had been warned not to drink anything I had made. Standing there in absolute shock, I asked him what he meant. He said my younger brother and his other daughter discussed their concerns – that I had been taking him off all his medications and was trying to heal him with my witch's potions. Tears filling my eyes, I left and got into the car, sobbing at the state he was in and the words coming from his mouth.

This stuff was available from fucking Holland & Barrett, not a cauldron in my kitchen. Never in a million years would I have ever taken him off any medication either. If anyone knew my dad, you

*would know he did what he wanted. He was no fool. It was his way
or no way.*

I had no numbers for anyone else. I called the occupational
therapist but got no response.

What could I do? There was no one else there for him that I
could contact. It made me feel ill. I felt full of guilt as usual. But
that is what he did; he caused upset and attacked those closest to
him. He'd done it for years to everyone.

I had to walk away. I'd hardly known this man, my biological
father, my whole life and now trying to build some sort of
relationship with him was breaking me. I did not know if he had
mental health issues or if this was just who he was. I decided to
step back from him. I was still reeling from the news about my
grandad who had supported me for years, and I was now
questioning everything he had ever done for me, wondering if it
was because of guilt. I had anger for my grandad for the first
time in my life and it left me shattered.

Later that year, the police interviewed my dad regarding my
case, and he said to the police SOLO, 'Tell Kathleen her daddy
loves her and to get in touch.' He was good at using emotional
words and knew he would get a reaction. Hating someone does
not come easy to me; I will forgive, and forgive … until I get to
a point and then I walk away still feeling for that person but
trying to save myself from any more pain. However, I did go and
visit him again.

By then I was pregnant again. I'd been in and out of
hospital and the doctor's for tests, and so I'd asked my dad
to get tested for the hereditary immune disorder that I had.
We'd visited the doctor's to get the result's. 'That came from
yer mammy's side, hen. Must have been yer granny that
passed it doon because she was always no well. Your illness is
not my fault either.' He was releasing himself again from any
accusations of faulty immune systems.

Never had I accused him of causing my illness. Despite the
fact that he – and many other relatives on his side of the family

– had been suffering symptoms similar to my own. That was the only reason I asked him to get tested; answers for everyone was all I wanted.

On the way back from the doctor's, my Dad needed to stop at the chemist and I waited in the car. His ex-wife and daughter walked by the chemist and spotted him in there. I watched as he had a chat with them, then gave them both hugs and came back to the car.

'I told them that I was thinking of going into a home, but you said not to,' he said.

WTF!

'No, what I said was don't go into the home that my cousin worked in as we had previously heard her talk about another relative and his drinking habits [you know who you are]. Your decision to go into a home or not is yours and yours alone.'

I considered contacting his ex-wife and daughter to get some of this stuff sorted but felt it was not my place to walk in after all these years and get involved.

My youngest daughter by this point had been going down on a Saturday to change his bed, clean the house and bring his washing to me. She also dropped off a few containers of food for the next couple of days if he was poorly. He would make comments to me about his bed not being made right and say, 'Tell her not to come down this week' – then call and ask where she was.

Fuck this, I thought. *You're not doing this shit to my daughter.* She was trying to build a relationship with him, but my older daughter wanted nothing to do with him at all. I told her he had a home help now and she could have her Saturdays back.

A while later he went on holiday and he called me, saying his medication had been stolen. I called the hotel and they said he had left it on a table and it had been returned to him. By the time he got home on the Friday he was still saying he had no medication. I offered to go to the chemist for him. He said he was fine.

By the Sunday night he pressed his alarm on his neck for an ambulance and by this stage he was struggling for breath. He'd not taken any medication for days and was refusing to use his nebuliser. The next morning, I got a text from him: 'I'm in the hospital again.'

Leaving my three-week-old son with a relative, I went to the hospital to see him.

He was lying on the bed trying to breathe; his eyes were sad, like a little lost child. He needed help. But sometimes I felt that he knew what he was doing, with the lies and manipulation of the stories he needed you to hear. Maybe this was part of the mental illness or brain damage he had. Maybe he was just a good con man. Maybe, just maybe, it was a cry for help, to be looked after and cared for. I was so bloody confused. I'd never experienced behaviour like this before from an adult, and I couldn't help but still try to care for and help him.

I walked away from him again after a while, disheartened and full of guilt but knowing that I did not have the will or tenacity to build a relationship with him again. My legal case was ongoing, I had a new baby and had little support. I had nothing left to give to him.

By bringing up my own past, others' pasts got stirred up, forcing them to look at their role in what I had experienced, and that was not comfortable for them. The best thing to do was leave, I thought. To stop causing anyone pain. My past was present and raw for me and I didn't want it to be disturbing or upsetting others.

My dad's sobriety had been a long journey too – something that I had never understood personally, but I would not jeopardise that either. He said that during AA meetings he had forgiven himself for his actions, but I knew he hadn't, not really. I knew when he saw my face and heard what had happened, it opened wounds up for him too. I had no stitches left for his wounds; mine had taken a while to be cleaned out and stitched up.

I hoped that he had everything he needed. He was a charmer, a joker, but he was never settled in himself. He helped a lot of people with their sobriety and their rights to benefits. His door was open to anyone. I just wished he had been like this with his own children from the start, but he had another side that could be vicious. He was a very complicated man to understand.

When I saw him on 4th December of 2012, he asked me to forgive him for not being there for me. I told him I had nothing to forgive him for. The past was a mix of many misunderstandings and decisions from lots of people. It was too late to say sorry now. The damage had been done.

Of course, I felt anger at his decisions – or lack of them – but I had no hate for him, just pity.

It was who he was. Knowing I gave it one last try to build a relationship was enough for me. Sometimes, family or not, people can have no place in your life if it brings devastating upset or sadness. Repeating cycles of behaviour that are toxic are not good for anyone; they only bring pain.

It takes courage to be selfish enough to put yourself and your children first. Not anger. I'm learning.

Dad, when I was a child I watched you as a father in another family: helping everyone you could … except me. I thought I had missed out on your love.

As an adult, I realised I had not missed a thing. You were so broken yourself that you could never have been any type of dad to me; that is fact. I merely missed what I thought you could have been. You never gave yourself a chance to be a better man or father. I am sorry you could not be braver for yourself.

'Father' – Demi Lovato: https://youtu.be/MZDAUbeSwNY

CHAPTER 23

Boxes Ticked

During 2014 a letter arrived from the solicitor, asking me to get ready to now see a psychiatrist for an opinion on my civil case (my case being against the social work department for totally fucking up). I was to be scrutinised – me – to work out just how fucked up and broken am I and what tier I went in for the damages to be paid.

Broken, damaged ... Box ticked.

When you open up about your trauma, you may hear something like this ...

This was so bad you cannot heal from it, you need help, counselling, behaviour therapy and it will all be fixed or managed. Your behaviour due to the abuse is not socially acceptable and it will almost lead to mental issues as well as physical issues. Your life will follow a pattern of triggers and repeated behaviour of anger, shame and risky decisions. You cannot hold down a job because you have issues with authority. You leave relationships or stay in abusive ones because you are so conditioned to that pattern of abuse.

No shit, Sherlock.

Disclosure is the best way. Go to the police, you get the help you so badly need, then get the attention that you never received as a child. You get believed by the therapists. Validation of what happened to you and tools offered to cope. The police prosecute this man and he goes to jail.

Fuck off, it's not that simple. This silver needle seems to come in so handy!

Let's say we have the visibly broken ones and the hidden broken ones.

Ask most adults who have been in this position, and one or the other option applies.

Can your innate sense of resilience and tenacity manage the pain in a way that is just as destructive internally, but at least no one gets to see your failure? Is it your sense of self, your higher self and age-old instinct for survival that gets you through daily? Is that different in all our journeys? Absolutely.

Does it also depend on your character and the relationships you built around you after the abuse also? Learning unconditional love from your children or having supportive friends/ husband? Being grateful for the small things and trying to see the positive, even in a day with nightmares or memories arising? Of course it does.

Everyone is different. Everyone's abuse and challenges were different, and so was how they were left feeling about what happened to them. So how everyone copes must be different too; it must be about them personally. We speak about individuality and characters, yet somehow we expect everyone that has been in this position to follow the same pattern and need the same treatments?

There is no box and no tag for me now because I have realised that boxes and tags only serve the people that want to place you there to make their jobs and lives easier. You are you, and you know what you feel. Never let anyone else negate that for you, never.

I have had tags growing up: 'The kid from care'.

I hid what was underneath and put on a face for the public and others around me – not the best coping strategy but one that was a little less destructive publicly and visibly. Would alcohol, drugs or prostitution have been any better? I cannot answer that. I have met others that like to feel numb, to forget and stay in that state for years.

The abusers and rapists depend on the after-effects of the abuse they dished out to keep you a victim. They depend on the horror replaying in your mind so they can accuse you of being mental, a liar and a fantasist, so they can rape you all over again on paper by dragging up your medical records, or attack your life and family should you ever attempt to try for justice.

Silenced, internal chaos, betrayed, worthless, damaged ... I have felt like all of these ... and then banished these toxic fuckers from my head ... Fuck off! I chose new things – happiness ... strength ... courage ... beauty ... freedom. I choose to stand in my own sovereign being, my higher soul, my internal power. I stopped replaying my hurt over and over and chose a path that was kinder to myself. The path continues ...

I own my pain; it's mine. I own my complex issues that other people caused at the very start of my life, and I have caused pain to others with this too.

I just manage it differently to try and thrive instead of just survive each day. I make the choice to be grateful, I trust my higher self, my body. I clear my energy, my chakras, my aura. It's a daily process but it gets easier. It's not a fucking hierarchy of who's the best healed victim or who had the worst experience.

'Historical' is only about the timeline, not the person's challenges, so when others think it is okay to state 'It's in the past, you should be over it', show them your back as you walk away.

Be aware that the reality of disclosure and the opening of old wounds is worlds away from the fantasy. It can be fucking awful and fucking beautiful in the same circle of crazy. I wish every other human in the same position as me the strength, courage and a voice and hope they try to find freedom from what they carry.

For the ones that had the balls to report, talk about or disclose – even on paper at the back of your drawer, this song is for you.

Redeem your soul from the box-tickers that weigh it down on its journey to enlightenment. Free yourself!

'Redemption Song' – Bob Marley:
https://youtu.be/QrY9eHkXTa4

CHAPTER 24

My Third Special Gift

After finally getting a diagnosis for my health in March 2013 through a specialist London doctor, my autoimmune symptoms had reduced considerably. I thought this improvement was down to the stress relief of having an answer at last, but it seems pregnancy suppresses autoimmune symptoms!

I was blessed with a third little Angel in 2014.

A boy!!!!!

Never in a million years had I thought that I'd ever have a son!!! I'm still grinning as I write this. He is my favourite. (Don't tell his sisters!)

He saved my life.

He saved many others, believe me . . .

My mothering instinct and my drive to be here for him and his sisters is much stronger than my anger and poor choices for revenge, of any sort, towards anyone else.

There are a few people that should be very thankful for this massive blessing. Divine timing . . .

To my wee favourite. (Don't tell your two sisters! x)

'How Long Will I Love You?' – Ellie Goulding:
https://youtu.be/an4ySOlsUMY

CHAPTER 25

Friends and Family

What can I say without offending anyone in this chapter? Really haven't bothered about that so far, have I? I was a lot more forgiving in my younger days, but these days zero fucks are given about your feelings or opinions.

I know where I have stood since all of this came out.

Let's list the reactions: I've been name-called, judged, ignored, tolerated, questioned, suffocated, controlled, ostracised … I could go on and on. But I will not let that happen anymore. It's the past. *You* are the past. Being alone has always been a part of my life. Not depending on others has been my constant.

I have my family, my three beautiful children, and I have real true friends – decent women who stand by your side, behind or in front of you when needed, who support other women, not bring them down.

I am surrounded by the most caring, strong and gentle love that I have ever experienced too …

To the rest of you who stood by and chose not to say what you could have said, who judged and made comments behind my back, who became distant because of the subject matter I was bringing to the fore. To the ones that did speak and chose to opt for something along the lines of 'Oh no, this again, she is mental, always a drama'.

If you are reading or hearing about this book and you want to connect again, don't bother. Lessons have been learned. Thank you for your place on my journey. I am on a new one now … and you're not invited.

'Wish You Well' – Sigala and Becky Hill:
https://youtu.be/1OK1OqA-En4

CHAPTER 26

Procurator Fiscal

It was 27th October 2014 and I was going to a meeting with the PF to discuss my case. I called over two weeks ago, yet again, for an update and this was the first appointment available for the 'decision'.

Two weeks of anxiety ensued, accompanied by the feeling it was not the news I was looking for. There had been no updates, no court dates, no feedback, fuck all.

I entered the interview room and on the desk were a file and a notepad. I could make out two words across the top of the notepad's page: *Insufficient Evidence.* So I knew the news right away, before the PF even opened her mouth.

She saw me look at the pad and I asked her to get straight to the point.

'Not going forward at present,' she said. NFA – no further action.

Scottish law depends on corroborating evidence. In other words, the statement given by me as an individual is not enough, and others failed to give one. The abuse and rape were historical so there was no DNA, no CCTV etc.

My stomach was flipping, I was shaking. I stayed as composed as I could in that moment in time. I asked what they had also considered, apart from my statement to the police, as in all the information that I had collated and provided for them:

- My victim statement;
- My social work files;
- The independent psychiatric report showing I was not bipolar;

- The story in the paper about PFB being headbutted in the groin while attempting to restrain a female patient that was standing up, and no one else was in the room with him.
- The update from me to tell them PFB had up and left Glasgow to be near his wife's family before this decision had been made. The PF never knew, nor did the police. There was still no outcome on the case and he had left Scotland and notified no one.

'It was there for their use,' she said.

Where the fuck was the support now? The transparency of the judicial system was not clear at that moment. Crown Counsel had made this decision on my case yet would not explain.

'We did our job. Please trust us,' she said.

You are kidding me? Trust really does not sit with me after the way I'd been treated over the past two years since I had come forward. I had been told PFB was going to court on 4th October 2013, but this never happened because the PF requested further information from the police.

I never knew that the PF could liberate the accused or cancel the undertaking unless they had decided that there was insufficient evidence in law, in which case no proceedings could be taken. I soon found out.

PF will contact police to co-ordinate the instruction of further enquiries [I only found this out in February 2014 in a brief conversation regarding evidence being picked up at my home.]

If insufficient evidence in law, then no proceedings can be taken. PF will liberate the accused from custody or cancel the undertaking. [No one notified me of this.]

Notification for Police to contact the victim as soon as possible. [Never happened!]

[This was researched from the Joint protocol between police and Crown Office and Procurator Fiscal Service.]

The PF had a few options to take:

1: *Proceed in the usual way with a summary prosecution following service of the complaint on the accused at court, the case could be dealt with that day if there was a plea of guilty.*

2: *move for the case to be continued on the strength of the undertaking without a complaint being served for further investigation or for consideration of diversion or offer of fiscal fine.*

3: *intimate before the case calls to the accused that the case would not call and arrange for a form of diversion.*

4: *intimate in advance to the accused that the case would not call and offer a fiscal fine.*

5: *intimate in advance there would be no proceedings.*

If the accused appears at court and pleads guilty or not guilty then the accuser would then be referred to the victim information service for support. They are there to give you information about the criminal justice system and keep you informed of the progress of the case and put you in touch with organisations that can help, give you practical and emotional support.

I did not qualify for this referral as PFB was never at court pleading guilty or not guilty.

If the PF decides to take no further action then you are entitled to information about the decision from the Crown Office and Procurator Fiscal Service. You can also ask for that decision to be reviewed.

Previously I had met with the PF for a precognition interview, where we went over my police statement. At this interview I asked for them to look at the complete social work file to see if there was any other information there as I was only privy to the piss-poor total of fourteen pages, and when I had asked them to make sure this was included with my victim statement letter to them, they had failed to reply too. My added letter explained the surrounding toxic environment of PFB's family and how he manipulated this situation for his own sexual benefits, and how sly and calculating his behaviour was. It outlined the fear and constant panic surrounding my existence, the mental torment and the physical abuse from other family members.

The PF made me aware of the solicitor's defence on behalf of PFB, pertaining to nude pictures of me.

It was a shoot for a family paper. It was for the women's section in *The Daily Record.*

It was a pregnancy wear shoot, combined with a few nude shots, my hand over my breasts, and my privates covered. They were classy pictures celebrating a woman feeling good about herself and her pregnancy, her body doing what a woman's body was designed to do. It was to show other woman you can embrace all the extra crazy things going on in your body in pregnancy. I knew why I'd done the shoot, but no one else would have understood why. It was a present to me from myself, for me to celebrate my body, to be free, to start healing. It was to give a great big 'fuck you' to PFB and his family.

I heard that the FS said she was upset that her father had seen these pictures in the paper and that it had nearly caused him a heart attack. Oh really? Was he shocked when he demanded I stripped my pants and trousers off and then leathered me with a belt, leaving marks all over me? I was naked then – was it okay in their own home, but how dare I do that in a national newspaper?

That made me laugh, that this was his legal team's angle of their 'defence', because if that was the only 'dirt' they had on me, then go ahead. I'm proud of my photoshoot. No one will ever dirty that time of my life or throw it back at me. My daughter growing inside of me was a blessing.

So, let's get back to the interview.

I asked, 'So if this is down to the basic law of corroboration and lack of evidence, then was that not clear when the police handed you the statements a year ago? Why not dismiss the case then, and not waste my time this last year on basic evidence that you have had since January?'

'It's not that simple,' she said.

She was fucking right about that, as I had no clue about their powers and the path this all followed, as no one had taken the time to explain it or guide me through the process at all.

Again, I asked what else they looked at for further evidence.

'I cannot answer that. Everything was there for their use,' she replied. It was like she was working from a script.

'So, can I now appeal this decision and have it relooked at?' I asked.

'No' was her reply. 'We will not intimate this to the accused. The case will lie open, and if further evidence becomes available, we will look at it again and we have the right to prosecute at a further time,' she said in her continuing script.

'So, if no one else knows that this is going on, how can they come forward for you to look at this again?' I questioned.

I got a blank stare from her across the desk, her face full look of compassion, like she'd been trained to do, no doubt.

What the PF failed to tell me when they advised me that they would not intimate this decision to PFB, what they never stated, was that they would, however, tell the accused or his solicitor if they happened to contact the PF themselves to find out what the decision was.

'There is one other thing I need to tell you,' she said. 'The NMC are looking to speak to you. Is it okay to give them your contact details? We can provide them your statement.'

This was her last gasp at giving me something positive out of this meeting.

The NMC is the Nursing and Midwifery Council, as in the governing body of Registered Nurses and Midwives. They have the power to strike off registered nurses if they see fit.

'Go ahead,' I replied. 'If it helps keep him away from others that are vulnerable, I will cooperate in any way I can.'

The tears were building up; I was losing my composure. This interview was a joke: no transparency, no answers, and fake empathy. The whole thing was very matter-of-fact and impersonal.

Fuck this!! My angry inner child was popping out to say hello again.

'So, if I go to the press and name him, what happens then?' I said.

The look of horror in her eyes at my statement said it all.

'That could affect your case,' she said.

I responded, 'What case? It's going to lie dormant. If I name him and someone else comes forward and gets justice then so be it. I'm getting nowhere for now.'

Because you know what, I believed I was never the only person to suffer at the hands of his depravity, and my gut instinct has never failed me yet. PFB worked with vulnerable mentally ill people. He then went on to work with those suffering from drug- and alcohol-related illness.

'Please speak to someone before you make that decision, Kate,' she stated.

'Yea,' I replied. 'I will make a call to the editor of the *Daily Record* – the same paper that printed my pregnancy shoot that was about to be used against me in a rape and sexual assault case from childhood as evidence of my character.' I rolled my head back in the chair. I was about to blow. 'Can I have this in writing from you, on paper, this decision?'

I asked for this because I had been called a liar, bipolar, mental, and FM had been going around telling people months before that 'this nonsense had been thrown out of court'. PFB had also moved out of the area well before then too; something stank badly.

Because of the nature of the allegations and charges against him, a social work order had been placed on PFB. He was not allowed to be alone with his wife's son. The social work department had no clue about the decision from the PF either but had not followed this up when PFB had moved out of their area before this decision was final. Social work following up on a child at risk? Fail!

The information spread about my case was lies, and you all know it. I have the letter stating the date the decision was made. Nothing was thrown out of court due to lack of evidence or lies.

No final decision was intimated to me until the date above: 27th October 2014.

'I will ask if that can be done,' she replied. I got up off the chair to leave.

'Please sit, Kate. We have someone from victim support outside if you want to talk to her,' she said, clearly noting my face full of anger.

No shit eh? Not one referral or ounce of support in two fucking years and now when you deliver your final blow you offer someone to chat to?

'She can fuck off too,' I replied, and I got up and I left.

I stood in the foyer of the PF office and pressed the lift button again and again, hoping this would make it come quicker. I needed out of here, back to my home with my family.

The whole way it had been handled from start to finish including the final meeting was a joke, in my opinion.

I arrived home, my tears wiped away, happy face back on. My wee family were all there with smiley faces for me when I got there. Their warmth and love enveloped me. I was home. It felt warm, comforting and safe. I was back to reality for a few hours until the kids went to their bed, but my head was spinning with how the whole process had gone, and I started to question whether it was worth it at all.

The police called that evening. The PF had called them and asked them to make sure I was okay, apparently. The officer that called was curious to find out what my next step was and asked me about my kneejerk reaction about going to the papers.

So, no one at all from the police had updated me on my case

in all this time, always redirecting me to ask the PF, but now here they were, all concerned about me going to the papers, on the same day I have the interview with the PF?

Interestingly, I recently found out that the police station I attended to give my statement and that made the charges had a certain member of PFB's family working there. This relative was removed whilst PFB was under investigation and charged, but even though I found the SOLO absolutely 100 per cent committed to doing her job professionally I now found myself querying the times when my SOLO was away or on a course and when others stepped in to answer my questions and give me updates and were less than productive. It was strange to me that the information they gathered lay on a desk for twelve weeks and never went anywhere, and it was strange that someone called and said they had not received it and could I give it to them again.

Despite my threats, giving my story to the papers was not my game. I wanted no part in being splashed all over pages of a newspaper and having some journalist spin the story. If this was ever going to become public, it would be through me writing about it.

So, after two years, I was another NFA (no further action), another statistic to be added to the long list within the Scottish justice system on sexual assaults and rape figures.

'Come forward,' they say. Be aware, be very aware, of the fantasy that the process is just you handing it over, and then it's done. It's not.

You need support, balls of steel and overflowing tenacity and patience. Don't expect the police and the PF to pat you on the back for being a good citizen and for bringing this to their attention, and then locking this person up. They work within a system of rules and law, and rightly so. But in law – and especially in Scottish law – there is corroboration. Check the statistics of sexual assault reporting and its outcomes first. Prepare for a long battle.

Not one person from the police or PF offered me any referral or support. Nothing at all through the two-year process, from my police statement right to the very end, when finally at the last moment I received a single offer of support. It was a case of 'Here is the bad news, someone is outside'.

Yet at the time of this ongoing saga there was the Victims Code for Scotland. It is there to inform victims of crime of their rights to:

- *Minimum standards of service, how you will be treated by organisations.*
- *Information, how you will be updated about your case.*
- *Participation, being understood and understanding what is happening and telling the court how a crime has affected you.*
- *Protection, feeling safe and protected from intimidation.*
- *Support, whether you report the crime to the police or not.*
- *Compensation and expenses, such as travel expenses, loss of earnings or compensation if you were injured.*
- *Complain, if you are unhappy about how an organisation has treated you.*

A previous attempt in my early twenties to try and report PFB's abuse was poorly handled. Now, in my forties, it seemed the system was not much better, from what I had experienced – for instance on my first call to the police, they could not tell me where my local Family Protection Unit was.

A victim's right to review within the one-month time limit didn't apply to me as the case hadn't been closed or dropped but rather was an NFA. It will sit on a shelf and if another witness were to come forward then the PF have a duty to look at it again.

I felt like this whole process was kept as far away from the public as possible, and further developments only seemed to confirm this feeling, but I cannot make any judgement on this without evidence, and without being sued for slander, so I will keep my opinion and gut instinct on this to myself.

There is however the Moorov doctrine.

The name Moorov is well known in Scottish criminal law. Samuel Moorov's case in the high court Glasgow in 1930 gave rise to this principle, which relates to the famous case from when Moorov, an Argyle Street draper, was accused of sexual offences against nineteen of his female employees over a period of about three years.

In short it means that several offences, each witnessed by only the victim of that individual offence, can be grouped together to show a pattern of behaviour and then that grouping could be used in a single court case.

A series of offences must be connected closely in time, character and circumstances and must have an underlying unity.

If any other witnesses come forward and make similar accusations against PFB, this principle can be used to bring him back to court. I will now have to wait and let the universe deal with this.

'Titanium' – David Guetta ft. Sia:
https://youtu.be/JRfuAukYTKg

CHAPTER 27

The Civil Route

I made an appointment with a solicitor to see if I had any redress against the social work department, which I felt had not done their job properly. I never knew family or social work law and what was in place to protect me in a foster situation, but I was going to find out and hope for someone to take some responsibility.

I was still awaiting my notes and went along for the first interview to be told that the time bar may be an issue. A time bar meant that anything that was not raised in under three years since the incident or three years after you become an adult, would not be heard. There were exceptions to that rule under specific headings and if you could prove you had been on drugs, a drunk or in a coma since that incident and you were now sober and aware, you might have got around it.

There is more to it than this, but this is my explanation of it simply.

I continued anyway and when I got my notes and a letter from my father from social work, things changed.

This timeline has been shortened so as I do not bore you as it is pages long.

Oh yes, every letter and movement were saved in order.

December 2012

Met with a solicitor.

After a long game of ping and a little bit of pong between myself and the other side, and lots of legalese I barely understood, I now have a date for my case to be heard in the Court of Session in Edinburgh ... Jan 2019, six years and one month from the first point of contact to the finish line. Within this timescale reports were undertaken, witness statements at the ready, but the other side seemed to not want to know or come to the table at any point. The time bar had been lifted in June 2017 so that could no longer be used as a way of deflecting me.

My understanding of the civil path was zero and I left it in the hands of the professionals. My assumption was that I would get a day in court to speak as a witness, armed with paperwork, legal reports of law at the time and witnesses galore to corroborate my story and the other side come and defend my accusations. The judge would then decide on this under law, record on paper and we have an outcome.

Foolish . . .

Get yourself a trusted firm of solicitors and advocates who keep you in the loop and do not try to confuse you with legalese or get caught out trying to call an intervention on you and your vulnerability when you question their path. Pick a firm that sees the person and not the accolade of winning or pay-out for themselves. Look at their other work, meet them and use your gut instinct. Save every single piece of paperwork you receive and ask every question you need to ask to keep yourself from feeling excluded from the club.

I had met two people from a firm at a meeting and really admired their manner, their compassion and their commitment so I approached their firm to help with my case.

They had a specific team assigned for cases like this and they managed my case well and with transparency and ease.

Within these six years I had no criminal case going forward so I was on this path now and would continue to keep going where I could in order to have this resolved.

I was looking for justice . . .

'The Sound of Silence' – Simon and Garfunkel:
https://youtu.be/f7McpVPlidc

CHAPTER 28

April Showers

It was 14th April 2015.

A letter from the Criminal Injuries Compensation Authority arrived. I had been awarded criminal injuries.

The award has been made on the balance of probabilities, based on the available police evidence, notwithstanding the absence of a conviction.

I felt like being sick. No justice. But hey, here's some money for you.

It knocked me sideways. To me this was 'dirty money'. Like the money PFB placed in my hand after the vile things he did to me.

I spent two weeks feeling out of place, and I never slept. This affected my health, and my immune issues flared badly.

April 2015 was the date that the abolishment of corroboration law in Scotland was to be heard – but on 1st April the headlines read: 'Plans to Abolish Corroboration in Scottish Cases Dropped'.

April 26th was my grandad's birthday. I battled with myself: I usually celebrated his birthday, but this year I was still holding anger and blaming him. I was angry at him for saying nothing about his involvement in my placement in care, and I was continuing to question his years of support. My trust had been shattered. If the one person you had trusted and depended on was full of bullshit, where does that leave you?

April was shit!

I had to dig deep and ask the universe to get me through this. It felt like a never-ending battle, and all I wanted to do was put all of this behind me and enjoy my family. I was ready to walk away and fuck everything off. This book was shelved too. My soul had apparently picked this journey and thought I was a fucking ninja, but at this moment in time I was losing faith in the last reserves of strength I had. I had to dig deeper.

'I Look to You' – Whitney Houston:
https://youtu.be/5Pze_mdbOK8

CHAPTER 29

HELP!!!

I have read lots of self-help books, trying every alternative therapy that I thought would help and while I have loved some of the therapies, I felt no 'fix', because that was what I wanted – to be fixed, because I believed I was broken.

Fear caused that for me. A lifelong existence in fear even after the abuse had stopped and I had moved away, time and time again trying to settle myself and find my home. It cost me my education and a business. It cost me friendships, jobs and relationships.

Everything I read or tried helped a little. I took a small piece of something from everything that I tried and I kept it for when it was needed. I educated myself on what the world and other people had to offer. I read worldwide respected authors and their books hoping the tools they offered would fix me.

The book lay back on the shelf and I was out of pocket and exhausted. Feelings of being let down and angry at this author, who was only offering what they had. How the fuck did they get this and I didn't? It's not fixing me! 'Bastards, I've just read your book and it's shit!'

There was my angry, hurt child, emerging again to have a rant. Have you ever said this stuff about self-help books? What does that tell you?

You were born with a gut instinct. You trusted your feelings, but then as you got older, as you suffered in any way, you lost that intuition, because reality, society, parents and events dictated that you do what they say. I lived on adrenaline with distrust, always waiting on the bad stuff coming again, even when things were good. There was an underlying thought that I never deserved happiness. I was always thinking, 'What's the catch?'

It's hard to go back to that state of self-trust, but it's your proper place. It's what connects your mind, body and soul. When you get there, you listen to it and you feel it.

So how did I get there, to this place? I lost my fear ... I gave it no more energy. I could not let it continue to rule my life anymore. It could not get any darker. I thought, 'Well, I cannot go any lower', so I asked the universe to help and handed over any control over this journey that I thought I had.

'Bring it on then, you fuckers!' I screamed to the moon. 'Do your best, because this is bigger than me.' I stood up in my garden and decided that I needed to do better and stop focusing on an outcome and enjoy what I had in front of me, be grateful for the place I was in.

Balance is the gift you can give to yourself: some ups, some downs, blend them together and do not beat yourself up.

That is all I can offer as advice; take it or leave it. You read this whole book thinking maybe, just maybe, I had a wee trick or tip, and you got nothing.

But always, always try. I felt a flow, a moving of energy and everything became clearer. That is the healing starting. It is the only way I can describe it.

All that fucking reading and payments for therapies that I used to constantly give up on was my lesson. This had to come from within, not from others.

We are all unique individuals with a different story to tell. That is why some guided work may suit some and not others. Simple really, a bit like diets! We see the 'celebrities' with extra weight, then training, then getting thin and a new DVD out lands in store. We buy it. We don't get the results then we say its shit. That's the result of wanting to be like someone else instead of you.

I hope you find your home within, where you started on this journey of your soul before the human experience landed and kicked you right in the face and then your arse as you bent over in pain. I feel very blessed and I will always remember where I was at, but I always balance that with where I am at now, how far I have come and the peace I give myself.

This song is for Katy, to remind her how strong she was as a child. My inner child is still here within me, up to mischief and the past pain is leaving. She's free. So am I!

'Run' – Leona Lewis: https://youtu.be/jqpAgMxhx30

CHAPTER 30

Walking Away from the Screams

Paedophile. The word is everywhere on newspapers recently.

You only have to glance at the news in the UK over the last decade to know that we have had an outpouring of reports of 'historical' cases of sexual abuse coming to the fore, with people in positions of trust being named and people coming forward after twenty or thirty years.

Physical abuse and sexual abuse within the care system is now under the scope of the enquiry in Scotland and England. Hopefully after all the changes and mess, the processes can move forward and give people some peace by being acknowledged.

Paedophiles at the BBC, the most well known being Jimmy Saville.

Jimmy Saville was the nice guy off the TV that all the kids wanted to be around. Like other predators he'd picked his environment for his own agenda. Remind you of anyone? Answers on a postcard please.

The term 'child porn' sickens me. Whether it be a picture or a video it's a record of a child being abused or raped, not porn. The papers sensationalise things and their wording is not only insulting, but it is lazy journalism and degrading to victims of crime.

Reports of sexual abuse in football seem to be better received by the public than those allegations against BBC icons or MPs. There seem to be no shouts of 'compo chaser' or 'liar' on this platform yet, like others have endured. Instead, a quiet nod of the head and a pitying look from others that this strong man was in this position. The way allegations made by men as opposed to women are received by the press and public is like black and white, but they are all damaging for those involved and their families, some of whom have been left distraught as some victims have taken their lives.

It's tough to hear and read when you thought you had started healing and now the can of worms opens further in your own living room or on social media or a newspaper.

I have taken a step back from any negative information until I sense that my brain can process it. I have decided to be grateful for everything I have and enjoy my family, the times at the beach, in bed with a book, eating and sleeping with no 'noise' from outside my circle.

Just like anyone else, I can't heal others in awful positions or fight their corners, nor should I try, but a big part of me really wants to care, to give a fuck about the state of our justice system. The low numbers of rape cases that get to the prosecution stage are a disgrace. The need to shout for other victims who have no voice lies behind my own path just now.

I have been to survivor group meetings and been to meetings aiming for changes to government legislation, and I've given my input regarding the time bar being lifted for abuse victims. I have contributed what I can at present. I don't want a sticker for it, or my back patted, but I was not comfortable in these settings, and it took a lot from me. There are others who are at home in that environment and make it their stage and shout very loudly, to do battle with clashes of opinion. I never needed another battle, so I stepped back.

My healing and the protection of my children must be first and foremost. Finding my balance and taking one thing on at a time is all I can do.

This is where I am more comfortable. In this book you are now reading. This is my contribution.

I am sharing my experiences and as much as it has been rough, raw and emotionally challenging for me as I typed each chapter, I purged myself of the lot of it and I am now laying down my sword and taking off my armour.

I'm now closing the book on the past and looking forward to a better future without battles.

For balance, for dark and light, yin and yang, to exist in a more peaceful place.

I have looked at where we as children lose our spirit, our gut instinct and our innate knowledge of being part of the universe and the bigger picture, and I have developed a tool for children to empower themselves. All children. Lavenderbuddy is a child's Bear filled with lavender and comes with 'I AM' affirmation cards, a backpack and a story book. When used daily it can help children to instil in themselves self-love, confidence, a voice, to be more mindful and kind, and to be brave. There is no online course, no constant parent needed for the journey. It is with them always as their friend and reminds them of the magic they hold within themselves.

If we as adults can build a strong foundation for future generations of children in a chaotic world full of power-hungry, lower vibrational systems, then we are doing our job as guides. This is my joyous, pretty contribution, a start on reminding children of their own power within, after the darkness of this book. From a vanity-published tale of misery lit mixed with some spiritual offerings to this below.

I thought I would describe my book as simple as possible before the critics jump on it ...

www.lavenderbuddy.co.uk

For now, I am being selfish. I have taken my 'wings' off my back, stopped being everyone else's angel and instead have put those wings on my wrists in ink, so I could see them every day to remind myself I come first.

Kathleen

X

Sam Cooke – A Change is Gonna Come:
https://youtu.be/wEBlaMOmKV4

The End. Or Is It?

Do you ever read a book to the end but then there is that tiny part of you wanting to know a little bit more?

Here you go!

My dad passed away in November 2015, the same month and day my grandad had died years earlier. He was cremated on 4th December, my mother's birthday. You couldn't make this shit up. There has been lots of this throughout this book.

I said my goodbyes to him at the hospital and attended his funeral with my head held high. There were some people who chose not to attend because I would be there. That's your issue. Keep it. It was about respect and a goodbye. Seeing family members again at the hospital and funeral was tough. I wanted to open my mouth and be vocal, but it was not the time or place. I'm sure this book will royally piss them off, so that will make up for me being graceful and not giving them another drama, as expected.

There was the usual family stuff that I have never had the breath to get involved in and there were people that made comments about how the funeral was arranged, who could come etc. To me, it was just logistics. I didn't want to be in a car. I didn't care where I sat, or care what food was on offer or who was invited. I don't do compliance with this mob anymore and I won't ever be told where to go, sit or be, by anyone from my father's family.

My father's youngest daughter took the role of planner and she did what she decided to do. She had been by his side consistently. Thank you. Your need to control and be recognised as his daughter and in charge was evident. I wished you well and walked away, as your path is very different from mine.

History likes to repeat itself with this family: my mother was not mentioned that day. The priest gave no reference to my dad's first marriage (to my mother). I am not aware if this was the priest's decision or whether he just read out what was offered to him on paper. But it felt like they were still pretending she didn't exist ... It never ends ... Cunts are always cunts.

There was a tiny moment of mischief in me that was going to stand up and interrupt the priest during the service, in the chapel, just because I could, but I chose not to. Amongst the silence and seriousness around me, I found myself laughing at one point, thinking of the drama it would cause.

I was there to say goodbye, and I did, with dignity and grace. I cried though, at the very end. After listening to my mother being shut out again, 'My Way' came on over the speakers at the crematorium. You couldn't have picked a better song for this moment. Yes, my dad did it his way, this whole team always had, no remorse shown for any damage done or people's feelings. People who attended were stopping at the exit to pay their respects and all I wanted to do was walk right out of there and stick up two fingers on both hands and shout that they were all hypocrites, but I never; I stood and looked them all in the face, even though mine was streaming with tears. I attended the wake in a local social club afterwards too and made sure I made my way round anyone that wanted to speak to me. I had nothing to hide – they were all aware I had reported PFB to the police and he had been charged. He never attended the funeral, and his avoidance of me says it all.

A certain number of people stayed in a table at the back, away from everyone, drinking their alcohol, even though it was a dry funeral as a token of respect to my dad's journey within the AA.

I'm sure that table had a card on it that was reserved for 'supporters of a lying rapist', but I can't be sure as I was not involved in the seating plan either.

Glasgow City Council and I had a date in January 2019 at the Court of Session in Edinburgh. I was looking forward to it. Instead – in an event that made me feel like I was reliving my teenage years, I got a 'dizzy at Boots corner' (a 'dizzy' being a local term for getting stood up, and Boots Corner being a junction of Argyle Street which was famous as a meeting place for dates). That is to say, Glasgow City Council settled out of court. I was naïve to believe I could have my say. Civil cases are mostly about the money for the people working on them, the best outcome being considered an agreement and money. Most things are about money nowadays, to be fair. You do wrong, you pay up.

Meanwhile, most people like me only want justice or an acknowledgement.

I never got the chance to have the council's wrongdoing logged on a legal piece of paper, never got an apology, no one took responsibility. The insurers covered it.

So, there are a few things I felt I needed to do:

1. Write this book.
2. Give a statement to the Scottish enquiry.

This way, something is on paper, to show the mess that was my placement into the council's care legally and the consequences it had on my life.

All done. Box ticked, and boy did I enjoy taking the pen in my hand for these boxes.

My grandad was accused of 'dumping us into the social work office', as my dad so brutally described it. This broke me. I battled between the states of loving the grandad I knew and trusted, and being angry and blaming him for not having the resources or knowledge to go back and fight to remove us from care after he had put us there temporarily. Until my older brother read a draft of this book and emailed me the following information.

Granda never gave you all away to the social workers.

Just before Ma died Granda was looking after our gran who was just out of hospital with a badly broken jaw. (ribs too) She was mad drunk in Springburn and got badly battered and robbed and spent months in Canniesburn hospital getting her face and jaw wired back together with operations. He looked after her as she was still bed ridden and could only take food by liquid/ powder. She was only out the hospital about 2 weeks when our Ma died. Ma died on the Saturday and social work came and took you all away on the Monday, the police were there too. You were all only meant to be away for a week or two we were told. Just until Granda could sort out our's and his house. I went up to [the children's home] *with Granda to pick you all up in a taxi and take you all home but he was not allowed to take you all out of there. They said that there was someone else that had put in to look after you all and that both parties now need to be assessed who would be best. That was the Monaghans not [FM] at first but [FM's mother]*

[FM] was pressured into it later by [FM's mother]. And an older head social worker called Mrs Mackenzie cut from the same cloth as [FM and FM's mother]. Dressed like them and was also a rabid Catholic, stern old school and emotionally cold. Her name will be all over the first social work reports on us and it will be down to her reports that no one from social work visited you all at first at (the first children's home), as she loved (FM and FM's mother) and had absolutely no time for Gran and Granda.

Granda went nuts at the home that day and on the way home and I remember being scared because he was frightening me with his anger that I had never seen before.

When we did go to visit you all in (the foster home) after it was done, (FM) said to him as we were leaving 'it's for the better they are here' and he told her 'you stabbed me in the back over these weans and you know it, they should never have been apart.' And same again all the way home angry and repeating over 'they stabbed me in the back'

　　Granda's only fuck up was that he trusted the social worker Mackenzie and trusted the Monaghans who both verbally agreed he would get us all together and both stabbed him in the back. He never ever forgot or forgave Mackenzie or any Monaghans and it hurt him deeply we were all apart. If anybody is to blame for you (sibling 1) and (sibling 2) being with the Monaghans it's that old malignant witch (FM mother) and that old bastard Mackenzie between them. And, our gran never helped his case with her drinking and her own madness.

Straight from the mouth of a then ten-year-old boy who watched it all unfold.

The relief I felt after I read this was unbelievable, and I was on the floor crying, saying, 'I'm sorry, I'm sorry grandad. I'm sorry I doubted you...'

This song is for my Johnny Fartpants! You did your best and I hope you are with my mum clapping away at my mischief and proud of me and my family. You always had my back and I am so grateful for that. My Thursdays have never been the same without you.

'Hurt' – Christina Aguilera: https://youtu.be/wwCykGDEp7M

To my mum, this book was a way for me to detail and bring to light the mess that has been left unsaid and covered up after you left this earth. For you to be acknowledged. Your image, the only photo I ever had of you, is on the front cover. Energy never dies and I know in my hardest times you were around even though I couldn't see you, but thank you for pouring strength around me, thank you for the two years we had. Your beautiful red hair I never got to see lives on in your grandson, a reminder every day of the family tree you birthed.

'You Will Never be Forgotten' – Jessica Andrews:
https://youtu.be/tRcJdzRrpCo

My journey continues along my healing path, and one of the ways I accepted was that there needs to be forgiveness in some way. Personally, as a spiritual being in a human existence, I found that so hard. So, I handed it over to my higher self and the perpetrators' higher selves to be dealt with in another place. Time will tell if this resolves my soul's journey and theirs.

The End!